Jaya Bhattacharji

—————
About the Author
—————

BABY HALDER continues to work as a maid for the employer who discovered her literary talent. Halder is writing a second book that continues the narrative of her life. She lives with her children in the outskirts of Delhi, India.

a life less ORDINARY

a LIfE LESS ORDINaRY

——— A MEMOIR ———

BaBY HaLDER

TRANSLATED BY URVASHI BUTALIA

Published by arrangement with Zubaan and Penguin Books, India

HARPER ⬤ PERENNIAL

NEW YORK • LONDON • TORONTO • SYDNEY • NEW DELHI • AUCKLAND

HARPER ● PERENNIAL

Aalo Aandhari, written originally in Bengali, was first published in Hindi translation © Prabodh Kumar in 2002. This English translation is based on the Hindi. *A Life Less Ordinary* was first published in English by

Zubaan
an imprint of Kali for Women
K-92, 1st Floor
Hauz Khas Enclave
New Delhi—110 016

www.zubaanbooks.com
in collaboration with Penguin Books, India.

FIRST HARPER PERENNIAL EDITION PUBLISHED 2008.

Designed by Kris Tobiassen

Library of Congress Cataloging-in-Publication Data has been applied for.

ISBN 978-0-06-137398-5

08 09 10 11 12 ID/RRD 10 9 8 7 6 5 4 3 2 1

I NEEDED TO LOOK IN A DICTIONARY TO UNDERSTAND the meaning of "dedication." But then it wasn't enough to merely understand the word; I also needed to know how you choose someone to dedicate something to and why you dedicate it to them. So I started to look at different books. Some were dedicated to friends and loved ones, some to sisters, others to fathers. I also found that there were writers who had written many books, and each one was dedicated to a different person. But I have only this one book—whom should I dedicate it to? I can perhaps dedicate it to someone I know, someone I respect. But if I choose one person, I may end up making another unhappy. There are so many people I could dedicate my book to, like my gurus, Ramesh Goswami, Ashok Prasoon Chatterji, Ashok Seksaria, Prabodh Kumar . . . but then I wonder, ought I to do that? If I do, they'll probably laugh at me, for more than being mine, this book is theirs. So then?

As these thoughts go round and round in my head, it strikes me that whatever I am writing now would not have been possible had it not been for my teachers, both the masters and the *didis*, who taught me the Bengali language and Bengali literature at school. This is why I have chosen to dedicate this book to them.

FOREWORD

by Urvashi Butalia

BABY HALDER'S MOVING AND BEAUTIFUL ACCOUNT OF her life has been almost constantly in the news since it was published in India, first in Hindi and then in a number of other languages. Baby—and that is her real name, although it probably began as a nickname (she does not remember being given a "proper" name)—is a young woman in her thirties, a mother of three. Abandoned as a young child by her mother, married off by an uncaring father to a man fourteen years her senior when she was barely thirteen, a mother by the time she became fourteen, trapped in a violent marriage, Baby's story is not unique. It is the story of thousands of women caught in similar situations across the world. What makes it different is Baby's strength and resolve; her determination not to stay in an abusive marriage, to make a new life for herself and her children; and, above all, her absolute commitment to the one thing she had always held close to her heart: the desire to read and write.

The story of how one woman escaped a life of hardship and poverty is what this book is about. But more than that, it is a book about reading, a book about books, a book about hope and despair. It is not a literary book: the writer is someone who almost learns to write as she goes along, whose prose goes from being sometimes staccato, sometimes stilted, to being fluent, expressive, and elegant. There is much about this book that may be puzzling for the reader who is not familiar with the world Baby describes, a world in which violence seems to be an almost routine, everyday affair. The voice that recounts this violence does so, similarly, without melodrama, without self-pity, in a curiously flat tone. There is also a vast network of relatives, a web of relationships that are both supportive and oppressive, sometimes moving from one to the other almost seamlessly.

Baby's account of her life begins with her childhood. As the adult eye looks back, we see a period that is at times idyllic and at times hard, but in many ways simply too brief. Before she knows it, she is thrust into marriage and adulthood, the transition from one to the other being marked only by the exchange of a dress for a sari. As her father and other relatives negotiate her marriage, Baby serves them food and drink, little knowing that it is her future that is being discussed. And then, exhausted from all the running around, she finds a moment to rest, and think, and her childhood passes before her: "Poor Baby! What else could one say of her? Imagine a childhood so brief, so ephemeral, that you could sit down and the whole thing could unravel in front of you in barely half an hour . . . Baby remembers her childhood, she savors every moment of it, licks it just as a cow would her newborn calf, tasting every part." The nostalgia for a childhood long gone disappears swiftly, however, as the narrative moves into an account of Baby's later life and leads the reader to the moment she makes the decision to leave. Finding her way to Delhi alone, frightened, two of her three children with her, Baby eventually manages to find a job, and the last part of her narrative takes the reader through the most exciting part of her life, when she begins by being a domestic worker in a home, and turns into a writer with a unique voice.

Baby Halder works today as a domestic worker in a house in Gurgaon, near Delhi. Her employer, Dr. Prabodh Kumar Srivastava, is also her mentor, and it is with his help that she has turned into a writer. Prabodh Kumar himself comes from a literary family. His grandfather, Premchand, was one of India's best-known writers, and his novels and short stories formed part of the great social upheaval of the early twentieth century and the movement for independence in India. Baby arrived at Prabodh Kumar's house one day in search of a job and began work as a domestic helper. Prepared to be more or less invisible, Baby was surprised when her employer actually spoke to her, asked about her life, and treated her like a human being. As the days passed, Prabodh Kumar noticed that Baby paid extra attention to his bookshelves, dusting and cleaning the books with care, looking at them with longing. And that was his signal for encouraging her, first to read and then to write. The result was the book you have in front of you, *A Life Less Ordinary* (published in Hindi and Bengali as *Aalo Andhari, From Darkness to Light*).

Baby's book came to my notice when I read a short report about it in a local magazine, and then on the web. The report mentioned that Baby lived and worked in a house in Gurgaon, and that the Hindi publication of her book had been received with much acclaim. Gurgaon is a large, sprawling urban jungle. Locating a domestic worker called Baby Halder in a city that large, that rich, and that anonymous was a task that was more or less doomed to failure. Domestic workers inhabit the shadow world of the nearly invisible people without whose help middle-class urban India would not be able to survive. But try to track them down, and you know you are attempting something that is virtually impossible. Yet in Baby's case we had at least one clue to go on, and that was the link with Premchand. For there were other members of Premchand's family who could be tracked down—the network of middle-class urban intelligentsia is a powerful one—and it was through them that I found my way to Baby, a young woman of enormous poise, wisdom, and compassion. Over time, Baby and I got to know each other, and her initial hesitation and concern about "the outsider" in her life gradually gave way to trust and the beginnings of a real friendship, and it is this that has formed the basis of my translation of Baby's story.

In a strange kind of twist, Baby's translator is also her publisher. At Zubaan, as publishers of books by and about women, our main concern has been to provide a platform where women's voices can be heard, where those who are on the margins can find the confidence to speak. But we know that it is rare, even for publishers like us who wear our politics on our sleeves, to be able to publish writers like Baby. Not only are they largely invisible, but many, indeed most, have not had the privilege of an education, and although they may feel strongly about issues, they often do not have the luxury of being able to give literary expression to them. For us, then, publishing Baby's book was enormously important: it is the kind of book that publishers like us dream about. It is a book from which we have learned a great deal, just as we have done from Baby, its protagonist and writer. And today, *A Life Less Ordinary* has become the international success that it deserves to be. For us, it also remains a book that we have been privileged and proud to publish, a book that has been inspirational in many small ways, a book that reminds us that there is so much that needs to be said and written about women's lives.

a life less ordinary

UNTIL THE AGE OF FOUR I LIVED SOMEWHERE IN JAMMU and Kashmir with my father and mother, my brothers and my sister. Baba, my father, worked there. It was a beautiful place with tall, high mountains and many different kinds of flowers. From there Baba took us to Murshidabad. After we had been there awhile, Baba was transferred to Dalhousie and we went to live there. Dalhousie reminded me a lot of Jammu and Kashmir. Snow would fall from the sky, the snowflakes swirling around like a swarm of bees, and settle gently on the ground. And when it rained, it was impossible to leave the house, so we would just play inside, or we'd watch the rain falling from our windows. We loved Dalhousie and we stayed there for quite a long time. We'd go out walking every day. We were so happy, just looking at all the flowers on the hillsides. We played all sorts of games among the flowers, and sometimes a rainbow would arch across the mountains, filling my heart with joy.

We wept when Baba took us to Murshidabad again, where my elder uncle, our Jetha, lived. Baba rented a house for us, and sent us children to school. Then he left us and went off to his job again. Every month he would send money home to cover our household expenses. At first the money would arrive regularly, but then, gradually, there were gaps of several months. Ma found it very difficult to make do: how could she not? After a while, even his letters began to arrive only after long gaps. Ma wrote letter upon letter to him, but there was never any response. Baba was so far away that Ma could not even go there. She was very worried, but despite all her difficulties, she did not let us stop studying.

Several years passed before Baba came home again. We were so happy to see him. But after a month or two, he was gone again. For a short while, he sent home money regularly, but then the same old pattern started again. Ma was so angry and frustrated that she often took it out on us. She asked our Jetha for help, but he was having a difficult enough time making ends meet for his own family. Meanwhile, Didi, my elder sister, was growing up, and that was another worry on Ma's head. Ma asked Baba's friends for help, but none of them was in a position to take on the burden of another family. Ma also thought of getting a job, but that would have meant going out of the house, which she had never done. And after all, what work could she do? Another of her worries was, what would people say? But worrying about what people will say does not help to fill an empty stomach, does it?

Then, one day, without any warning, Baba turned up. Ma burst into tears when she saw him. And all of us began to cry, too. My Jetha and others in the neighbourhood tried hard to explain to Baba that going off like this was not the right thing to do, but he did not seem to be convinced. He just left Ma and went off again. She was in a terrible state. I was a little better off than she because at least I had some friends, especially Tutul and Dolly, whom I could always talk to and who loved me a lot.

A short while after Baba left this time, he wrote us a letter to say that he'd soon be retiring and coming back home. We were overjoyed, but when Baba eventually came home, he did not seem at all happy to have retired. He would not speak to us or to Ma properly, and he'd lose his temper at the smallest things. We were a little frightened of him, and now we began to keep out of his way—whenever we saw him coming, we would creep away.

Didi was growing up, and Ma could not stop worrying about her. One day my younger uncle from Karimpur wrote to say that he had found a possible match for her. As soon as he read my uncle's letter, Baba quickly packed a few things, took my sister, and, without saying anything to anyone, left for Karimpur. Ma was really upset. She kept saying she couldn't live like this anymore. When, she asked God, would she have peace in her life? Suddenly it all became too much for her, and one day, with grief in her heart and my little brother in her arms, she just walked away from home.

At first we thought she'd just gone to the market as usual. But when she didn't return even after a couple of days, we realized that something was amiss, and all of us began to cry. Our Jetha, who lived nearby, tried to reassure us, saying that perhaps she had gone to visit her brother and would be back soon. Baba was in Karimpur when she left and four days later, when he came back, he asked us what she had said before leaving. We told him she had said she was going to the market. He then went to her brother's house in search of her, but she wasn't there. He searched every place where she could have possibly gone, but there was no trace of her. He was completely at a loss—he'd looked everywhere and was now really worried because there was nowhere else to look.

Finally, someone suggested that he should consult a faith healer and see if he could help. And so Baba set off in that direction. He kept doing this: someone would suggest one thing and he'd go off and do that, and someone else would suggest something else and he would turn around and do that. But he must have known—just as all the people in our neighborhood had perhaps guessed—why she had left. And everyone blamed him, saying she wouldn't have left if it had just been a question of a little bickering. These things upset us a lot, but there was not much we could do. Baba was also unhappy. These nagging worries had changed him a lot. He was also very concerned about Didi. How could a grown girl be kept at home once the mother had gone? Didi wasn't even that old—just fifteen or so. But Baba wasn't willing to wait, and he just married her off so that no one would have anything left to say.

It was only after Didi went away that we realized how difficult things could be without a mother. When the moment had come for Didi to leave, she'd cried, saying that if Ma had not gone, we wouldn't have had to shoulder this burden. "You're sending me off," she told Baba, "but now the responsibility of looking after these young children will be yours. They have no one else to call their own." Didi left and our problems began in earnest. Baba never stayed at home. Sometimes he would give us money and tell us to get ourselves something to eat. But he would still say: "Whatever you do, don't forget to study."

That was why, in the midst of all this hardship and trouble, we never stopped going to school. I had a good friend in school whose mother often called me home and gave me something to eat, and even asked me to stay with them. Our school headmaster was also very kind to me. He gave me notebooks and pencils, and after Ma left and our tuitions stopped, he got his daughter to give me free tuitions.

I loved school as much as I hated home. I never wanted to go home—there was no one there who appreciated my work in the same way as my teachers at school, so there was no incentive for me to go back. The days when there was no school stretched out forever, and I missed Ma and Didi terribly, so whenever I got the chance, I'd run off to play with my friends. I used to love playing games with them! We played *kit-kit*, *lukochuri*, and *rumalchuri* and skipped to our hearts' content, and the hours would just melt away.

I never missed a day of school, and often people did not know that I'd come to school without having eaten a thing. I was too scared of Baba to tell him there was no food. One day a friend of mine came to our house to fetch me so we could go to school together. I quickly got ready to go. My friend told me I should eat something before we left, and I blurted out that there was nothing in the house to eat. Baba heard this. I didn't know he was at home, or else I would not have said anything. That day, when I came home from school, he beat me so badly that it was three days before I could get up and many more before I felt able to go back to school again. My teachers and friends came to ask after me.

As soon as my brother was a little older, he decided he could not live with Baba, and so he went to stay with my aunt. Once he got there, he realized that she wasn't too well off, either, and was only just managing to scrape by herself. At home now there was only Baba, myself, and my younger brother. Our Jetha thought the best way to put our family back together again was to get Baba to remarry. When he first suggested this, Baba resisted, but very soon he came around to the idea.

My stepmother never listened to anything Baba said. She never fed us on time, she often beat us without reason, and she'd cook up tales about us and tell Baba and we'd get beaten by him as well. Baba was not willing to listen to anything we had to say, and there were times when he would refuse even to look at us. There was nothing we could do. When Jetha realized what was going on, he called Baba and explained to him that before he punished the children he should at least try to find out whether they were at fault. After being told this, Baba began to change. He began to realize that not everything our stepmother told him about us was true. But then, the moment he began to question her, things became much worse at home. Whenever things became unbearable, he would take her to her brother's home and leave her there. There her father and brother often tried to reason with her, but the moment she came back to our home, everything was the same again. She would not feed us properly, nor treat us well. Things got so bad that sometimes we—and even Baba—were forced to try to cook our own meals. Since we were still so small, we would sometimes burn our fingers in the process. While all this was going on, Baba started something—a business perhaps—that took him away from home for two or three days at a stretch, but the moment he returned he'd have to listen to our tales of woe about not being properly fed or looked after.

Days and weeks and months went by like this, and then suddenly one day Baba announced that he had to go to Dhanbad for an interview for a driver's job. He told Jetha he was going and he came back a month later. He was only at home a few days before he was off again, leaving us in Jetha's care. And this time he was away for many months. He didn't send us any money, either, and we were in real difficulty. He turned up out of the blue one day and took us both and our stepmother to Dhanbad, where he'd been given a place to stay. My brother and I were sent back to school. He did not bother to buy us books and notebooks, but we managed somehow. I loved school and worked hard. Perhaps that is why I had so many well-wishers there. I don't quite know how Baba spent the money he earned, but I do know that he used to drink, and that this had become much worse after my real Ma left.

We'd been in Dhanbad only a few days when Baba got a job in a factory in Durgapur. So he left us with a friend who was like a sister to him and went off to Durgapur. Even though she wasn't a blood relation, she was really good to us, but when the money Baba had left with her for our expenses ran out, she became very worried. What would she do now? After a lot of thought she decided it would be best to send my brother and me to her father, and to send my new Ma to her brother. By the time she made this decision, Kali Puja had come round. On Puja night, everyone wore new, colorful clothes to celebrate, and there was a general atmosphere of festivity. But not for us. My brother and I sat on our doorstep and watched all this, and we cried.

I was really angry with Baba. Because of him we had to listen to all sorts of things from people. They would say things like, "Even though you have parents, you might as well be orphans"; and "Your father works somewhere far away, and that's why you are in this state"; and "If you don't have a mother, you have no one!"

Baba came back a few days after Kali Puja. It was the middle of the night. We were all asleep, but when we heard his voice we woke up with a start. He called us to him and gave us the good news that Ma had returned, and it made us so happy. I asked him again and again where she was, and he said that if you both want to meet her you will have to come with me now. He then told our new Ma a lie. He said, "I am going to your father's house. Tomorrow morning, take the train and join me there. I don't want to delay things any further right now. There are also some people I owe money to." He added, "If they see me they will demand to be paid and I don't have any money, so it's best to leave quietly." He lied to her like this and took us with him and left. When we got to Durgapur we found that the woman Baba was calling our mother was another mother altogether. I said to my brother, "How much more do you think we will have to bear?" and he began to cry. Our third mother could not bear to see him cry, so she gathered him in her arms and began to soothe him. That made me think that perhaps we would get love from her, but the reality that unfolded was quite different.

Baba would not let our third mother out of the house: she wasn't even allowed to go to the tap to fetch water. If water was needed, we were sent out for it. And we were so frightened of Baba that we did not dare say anything. The people in our neighborhood felt very sorry for us, but they, too, could not do anything. This mother's sister, that is, our aunt, was a very simple and loving woman. She cared for us a lot. Sometimes she would take us to her home, but Baba did not like that. She tried to tell her sister to treat us better, but our third ma said, "What can I do? I'm only following their father's wishes." We used to think that she, too, did not like her sister taking us away to her home.

Baba had brought us to Durgapur, but he did not say a word about us starting school again. I had become so used to going to school that once all the household chores were done, I would go off anyway with other children from our neighborhood. But Baba was not happy about this. One day one of the girls from our neighborhood saw me standing at the edge of our road and crying. She told Baba. He came and asked me why I was crying, and through my sobs I told him that I was really missing Ma and asked why he had lied to us about her having come back. This ma was not our real ma . . . Baba's eye suddenly fell on the coin I was clutching in my hand, and he asked me what it was. I had to tell him then that it was the ten-paisa coin Ma had pressed into my palm the day she left and that every time I saw it I remembered Ma.

Baba felt very bad at this. Gently, he asked me what my brother and I wanted. I said I wanted to study. A few days after this Baba sent me to Jetha's house, saying I should stay there and that way I could carry on with my studies as well. But he never once considered that Jetha did not have a lot of money to spare, that his health was not particularly good, and that it would be unfair to impose this burden on him. Once there, I realized there was no way I could carry on studying, so I decided to at least seek out my old school friends. First I went to see Tutul. She had just come back from school and was really happy to see me. I used to call her mother Kaki-ma, and when she saw me, she welcomed me and quickly cooked some food for the two of us. Kaki-ma's kindness reminded me of my own mother and my hand stilled while eating. When Kaki-ma asked if anything was the matter, I told her that had my mother been there, she, too, would have fed me with the same care and love. Kaki-ma merely said, "Yes, child, but what is to be done? It's your fate to not have a mother even while you do have one."

After eating, Tutul and I started chatting, and then we went off to meet our other friend, Dolly. Dolly was a beautiful Brahmin girl and our fathers knew each other. One day, when Dolly's father asked me about Baba, I gave him all the news and also told him everything about myself. Dolly's Baba talked to the school headmaster, who knew me because I had been a student in his school. I was really happy when he told me to start coming to school the next day. And so I started at school again.

But now another problem came up. Because I was now living in Jetha's house, my third ma found it really difficult to cope with all the household tasks. And one day she and Baba arrived at Jetha's house to take me away. Jetha refused to let me go, saying, "She's going to school and doing so well, I will not let her go away." But Baba insisted and said all kinds of terrible things to him. In the end, Jetha gave in, but he told them that if they made me unhappy there was no way they would get any happiness themselves.

They took me away from Jetha's house, and once again my studies stopped. Now I thought of only two things: whether I was asleep or awake, my thoughts would constantly turn to my studies and my mother. I had heard that excess of worry makes people ill, and sure enough, that happened to me. Baba took me to a hospital, but the doctors were unable to diagnose my illness. This worried Baba, and he called in another doctor. I told the doctor everything that had been worrying me, and he was very angry with Baba, and scolded him.

Gradually I got better. One day, while I was still in the hospital, I woke in the morning to find my bedsheets wet with blood. I was frightened and I began to cry. The nurse heard me and came to find out what was wrong, but I was so scared I could not say anything to her. But then she noticed the sheet and asked me if anything like this had happened to me before. I said no, and she understood the reason for my fear. A few people had gathered there and they were all smiling. Patients in the other beds tried to explain to me that there was nothing to worry about, that this happens when girls grow up. The doctor came and told me I was well now and could go home. I begged the nurse to allow me to stay on for a few days, but she said there was nothing wrong with me, and that all would be well if I followed her instructions.

Baba came and took me home. When my new Ma saw me, I thought she looked a little concerned. I went in for a bath and when I had finished I saw her looking at my bloodstained clothes. I told her what had happened in the hospital and then I thought she was telling Baba something—he looked a bit worried, too, although he did not say anything. In fact, every time I looked at him, it seemed that he was thinking about me, but I did not have the courage to ask what was on his mind.

NOW, ONCE AGAIN, I BEGAN TO WORRY ABOUT MY STUDIES. Perhaps Baba understood what was in my heart, although he did not say anything because he knew that my new Ma would not want him to talk to me about it. I was constantly surprised by her behavior. At times she would be so loving toward my brother and me, and then suddenly we would become the cause of tension and conflict between her and Baba, and the whole house would become a battlefield. Baba's behavior had changed, too. He no longer scolded me, and if I did anything wrong or made any mistakes, he would simply say, "You're not a child anymore. You should be more careful." He told me so often that I was no longer a child that I began to wonder if perhaps I had grown up after all.

Slowly, I began to see signs that told me this indeed was so. One day I was sitting on the *chowki*, reading aloud, when I suddenly looked up and saw Baba watching me intently. He was listening carefully to what I was reading. When he saw me looking at him he asked me if I would like to go to my aunt's house. I made no answer. I don't know if he thought I was being rude, but he did not say anything. Earlier, if I did not reply to something he asked, he would sternly tell me off.

I think the boy who lived in the hotel behind our house, like Baba, had also begun to think I was now grown up. Every time I sat down to read in the room, I would find him watching me from his window. If I went to fetch water from the tap outside, he would come and stand there and watch me. One day I noticed him talking to my brother and pointing at me. I think he was asking about me. Another day I saw him asking a friend I used to play with about me. She came and told me afterward, and asked, "Why does that boy want to know everything about you?"

"What's so strange about that? Everyone here wants to know everything about everybody. But don't tell Baba about him—otherwise he'll beat me up." She kept smiling at me as if she knew something I didn't—that's why I had to add that.

This friend of mine was named Krishna. She was short and fair, with a slightly crooked tooth, but she was still good-looking. Her sister, Mani, was also lovely. The three of us took tuitions together. I remember that one day there was no electricity and we were sitting and studying by the light of a lamp. I tried to move the lamp a bit and the hot glass brushed against the teacher's knee! I was scared to death! *Now he's sure to tell Baba and then I'll get a beating,* I thought. But he did nothing of the sort. He just kept quiet. But even though he did not give the incident any importance, Krishna and Mani kept reminding me of it and teasing me.

They must have also told their father about me, for one day their Baba and mine talked a lot about me and my brother. Their father asked Baba why he did not let his children be children. "Why do you keep scolding them all the time?" he asked. "Why don't you let them play when they want to? You're always stopping them playing, or going out if they want to . . . They're still children, after all: do you have to keep them busy with household chores all the time? Don't you think they want to go out and play, like all children do? Your daughter is so scared of you that even when she is ill she dare not tell you. And anyway, what good would it do even if she does? She also knows that. Tell me: is this right?"

Krishna's father was not wrong. When my mother left, she took all the joy in our lives with her. Baba did not allow me to wear bangles; I wasn't allowed to talk to anyone, to play with anyone, and often not even allowed out of the house. I was so scared of being beaten that I would look for opportunities to go out and play only when I knew he was not around to stop me. I was only eleven or twelve years old at the time, and I used to think that no one could be as unfortunate as me. I used to think that only I knew what it means to lose a mother. Sometimes when I thought about Ma, I would think that if it had been Baba who had left instead of her, perhaps things would not have been so bad. After all, what had Baba given us, except fear? I used to think that perhaps there were no children who feared their own father as much as we did. His appearance, with his round, plump face; his tall, solid frame; and his huge moustache, did not help. He frightened everyone away—other children were scared even to come near him!

I longed for my mother. I used to think that if only I could have her love and support, my fear of Baba would be manageable. Had she been around, I would not have had to abandon my studies: of this I was sure. She wanted so much for me to study. In fact, had it not been for her, and her support and constant encouragement, I would not have studied even as much as I had. It was only now that I was able to appreciate how important it was to be able to read and write. The years I had spent at school had taught me that much at least. History was my favorite subject. I loved it and really enjoyed it, and perhaps that was why the history teachers also liked me. They used to tell us about different battles, about the Rani of Jhansi, about Nawab Sirajudowlah, about all sorts of kings and queens and nobles. I often wished I could meet all the people whose stories we heard. I would have liked to have talked to them. And whenever I studied history, I would remember my mother. I don't know why . . . I just did. Maybe it was somehow connected to the things that our neighbors used to say about us— about how such a well-knit family had fallen apart with just the departure of one person. Or perhaps it was that Rani Lakshmi Bai's story—about how she took her little boy and fled with him on her horse—reminded me of the day Ma took my little brother and left us. But then I thought, *What's the use of wondering and speculating?* History reminded me of Ma, just as women walking down the road did, and that was all.

Baba also kept on searching for Ma. Every time he came home from somewhere, the first question we asked him was whether he had any news of Ma. He'd say, "No, child," and then he'd let out a long sigh. I felt very bad for him at such times. I thought that finally he was beginning to understand that if he had not treated her so badly, she would never have left. And yet he was the same father who seemed so happy when our new Ma came into the house. It was difficult to tell whether he was really happy or not.

It was a few days after Krishna's Baba had talked to mine that Baba called me and asked if I wanted to live at my elder aunt's house. At the time I had not answered. Shortly afterward, I heard him talking to my new Ma. They were talking about my marriage. I had no idea what marriage was. All I knew was that it was an occasion for song and dance, that often lots of people went to marriages and had lots of fun.

I had only one elder aunt, and she was very fond of me, so even though I had not answered when Baba had asked me if I wanted to go and stay with her, when he did send me there, I was very happy. My elder brother was already with her—he was working in a large restaurant. I stayed at my aunt's home for some months, and those days passed well for me. My aunt would take her daughter and me out somewhere every evening, and every night she would tell us stories. It was while listening to a story of hers one night that I was suddenly reminded of a funny story that my friend Dolly used to tell us. I started to laugh, and my cousin asked me what was so funny. When I told her, she insisted that I should tell her the story. And I was keen to tell it as well, so I said to her, "Okay, so listen . . ."

Once upon a time there was a jackal and a village headman. The headman's garden was full to overgrowing with aubergines. When the jackal saw the aubergines his mouth began to water, and he began to wonder how he could get at them. There was a fence of thorns surrounding the headman's garden. But the jackal just had to get to the aubergines. He began to imagine what would happen if he ran back and took a running jump into the garden. He was just about to try when the headman woke up and, frightened, the jackal ran away. After this, the jackal would go to the garden every day, looking for an opportunity to jump in, but would return in the evening disappointed. One day, as he was passing by the headman's house, he saw the headman's wife making *pithas* and her husband sitting there eating them, one after the other. The jackal hid and watched him. Once he's eaten, the jackal thought to himself, he will surely go to sleep . . .

I had only gotten this far when my aunt sternly told us to stop chattering and go to bed. But my cousin insisted that I finish the story. So I said, "Okay, listen again . . ."

The jackal had thought that the headman would eat his fill and sleep soundly. And that is exactly what happened. Overjoyed, the jackal took a running leap to get to the aubergines and . . . fell hard on the fence of thorns. Thorns stuck into his paws, his legs, his whole body—and he fell to the ground bleeding. Instead of gorging on aubergines, he spent the whole night picking thorns out of his skin. Come morning, he was still hidden from the headman, picking out thorns, but no matter how hard he tried, there was one stubborn thorn, stuck in his ear, that he could not pull out. Finally, when he could bear it no more, he went to the headman's house, crying, "Brother, are you there? Are you there?" He began to bang on the door.

The headman asked, "Who's that at this unearthly hour?"

"It's me, Brother, the jackal."

"What's wrong? Why are you knocking at my door so early?" the headman asked.

The jackal said, "Please come out."

So the headman came out, and what did he see? The jackal all covered in blood.

"What happened to you, jackal?" the headman asked.

"Don't ask, Brother . . . I tried to get into your garden to steal aubergines and . . ."

The headman was furious. "Why are you disturbing me now?" he snapped The jackal told him that he'd spent hours pulling out thorns but there was one stuck in his ear that he just could not reach, so he'd come to the headman for help. The headman was angry anyway that the jackal had dared to get into his garden to steal, so he thought, "Let me teach this fellow a lesson."

"All right, but what if your ear gets cut when I'm taking out the thorn?" he asked.

"No matter," the jackal said, "if my ear gets cut, at least it will be for a good cause."

So, instead of pulling out the thorn, the headman cut the jackal's ear in that exact place. The ear began to bleed, but the jackal did not say anything. Just as he was about to leave, he turned and said, "Brother, you have cut my ear, now what will you give me in exchange?"

"I have nothing to give you," the headman said, "but if you like you can take this spade for digging."

The jackal took the spade and left.

On the way he met a farmer who was scraping at the earth with his hands. The jackal asked why he was using his hands, and the farmer replied that he had nothing else. "I have this spade," said the jackal. "I can give it to you, but you will have to give me something in exchange." The farmer took the spade and said to the jackal, "I have nothing to give you. All I have is this staff that I use for grazing the cows. Would you like it?"

"Why not?" said that jackal. "I'll take it."

Halfway through the story my cousin said, "It's getting late. Let's go to sleep now—we'll hear the rest of the story tomorrow." I asked if she would remember the story so far, and she said yes. Then both of us went off to sleep. We woke late in the morning to a scolding from Aunt, who told us off for oversleeping, and warned us to sleep on time that night and not to spend our time chatting. But that night, no sooner had Aunt left us than my cousin said, "Okay, now tell me the rest of the story, but make sure you whisper so she does not get to know that we are awake." I asked her if she remembered where we had left off, that the jackal was about to take the farmer's stick in exchange for his spade? "Yes, yes," she replied. "Now get on with the rest." So I said, "All right, so listen . . ."

The jackal took the staff and went on his way. A short distance later, what does he see but a peasant using his bare hands to chase a cow away! So he asked, "Brother, what are you doing?"

The peasant said, "This cow is eating up all my grain, so I am trying to make it run away."

"But how can you do that with your bare hands?" the jackal asked. "I have this staff . . . would you like to take it?"

"Why not? I'll take it."

So the jackal gave it to him. "Will you give me something in exchange?"

"But what if the staff breaks?" said the peasant.

"Well, what if it does? At least it will have been put to good use."

The peasant said, "But I have nothing to give you . . . except, wait. I have this small shovel."

"All right," said the jackal, "give me whatever you have." And so saying, he took the shovel and went on his way.

A little further along, he met another farmer who was digging mud with kitchen tongs. When the jackal saw him he asked, "Is this all you could find to dig with?" The farmer replied that he had nothing else. So the jackal said, "I can give you this shovel if you like."

"Okay, give it to me," replied the farmer, "but what if it breaks?"

And once again the jackal said, "Well, so what? At least it will have been put to good use."

When the farmer began digging, the shovel broke into two pieces.

"Hey, Brother, why have you broken my shovel?" said the jackal. "Now you'll have to give me a new one or give me something else in exchange."

The farmer said, "You may have lost your shovel, but other than these tongs I have nothing to give you. Please take these if you wish."

The jackal took the tongs and headed off again. Suddenly he felt hungry. In the distance he spied a house and headed toward it. He saw a woman sitting by the stove, stirring rice with a stick. "Sister, what are you doing?" asked the jackal. "I am very hungry. Please give me some of that rice you are cooking." The woman turned to her husband: "Just look at this jackal! The food isn't even ready yet and he wants to eat!"

"She is right," the jackal told the man, "but what can I do? I'm dying of hunger."

"Well, just have a little patience," the wife replied, "the food is nearly done."

Then the jackal and the man and woman all sat down to eat together. After they'd finished, the jackal said, "I have eaten so well, but I have nothing to give you other than this small thing." The husband asked to see what it was, so the jackal showed him the tongs, saying, "This is no use to you, but it might come in use for your wife." The woman took the tongs happily.

"You've got something useful," said the jackal, "but what about me? Do you mean to send me away empty-handed?" To this the woman replied, "My husband has a drum . . . would you like to take that?" The jackal said, "All right, give me that." He took the drum and left, and he was happy that in the end he had found something he wanted.

All along the way he beat the drum and sang:
I went to eat aubergines and I left behind my ear,
in exchange for the ear I got a spade,
tak duma dum dum dum dum,
in exchange for the spade, I got a stick,
tak duma dum dum dum dum,
in exchange for the stick, I got a shovel,
tak duma dum dum dum dum,
in exchange for the shovel, I got some tongs,
tak duma dum dum dum dum,
in exchange for the tongs, I got a drum,
tak dum dum dudum dudum.
And singing away, he made his way home.

By the time I got to the end of the story, I was quite sleepy and I nodded off. Sometime later, I awoke and I don't know why, but at that moment, a memory powerfully came back to me of the ten-paise coin my mother had pressed into my palm the day she had left home. One day my aunt took that coin from me and threw it away. After that, I searched high and low for it, but it was nowhere to be found. I was just thinking about this and wondering what my aunt had done to the only thing my mother had left me to remember her by when I was startled to hear a slight noise. I looked to see what it was and found that my cousin was talking in whispers with someone outside the room. Then it seemed as if she went somewhere. After a while she came back and quietly lay down next to me. I looked toward the window to see how late it was when I saw a boy standing there. He shone his torch into our room, and I quickly closed my eyes lest he should see.

After that, I couldn't get to sleep at all. In the morning, I wondered if I should tell Aunt what had happened during the night, but then I felt scared. I thought, *What if she says something to me instead? What would I do?* After a lot of thought, I decided to stay silent. But I was dying to tell someone: that secret kept flapping around inside me! In the end, when I just couldn't keep it in any longer, I told the whole story to two sisters, Sandhya and Ratna, who lived next door to my aunt. They advised me not to speak of this to anyone. "She's your aunt's daughter," they said, "and she will not say anything to her, but she may just turn around and accuse you of something. You'd better be careful. She knows you have no one to speak up for you and take your side."

After what happened that night, I felt very depressed and I increasingly felt the need to go away, at least for a short while. When I told my aunt this, she asked me where I wanted to go. I said, "Maybe to my sister's home? Just for a couple of days?"

"But what if your Baba comes to pick you up when you're not here? What will I say to him?"

"What's the problem? He can just as easily collect me from his elder daughter's home, can't he?"

So then she asked her son to take me to my sister's house.

When I arrived and my Didi saw me, she began to cry. She kept saying that she had no mother, she had no one and none of us cared for her. I realized she was not happy in her marriage, but I put that thought out of my head and took her little baby into my arms. Didi told the child, "Look, this is your aunt." We had heard that Didi had had a little boy, but Baba had not gone to see her after the child's birth and he had not allowed us to do so, either. "If Ma had been around, she would have dropped everything and come to see me and her grandchild," she said.

Didi and I were talking when her husband came back. He gave a shout of joy when he saw me. "Oh, Sister-in-law! I thought you had forgotten all about us!" His voice brought the rest of the household out, and in no time at all we were laughing and crying and talking all at once.

I spent a whole month with my Didi and the time passed very well. Didi's brother-in-law would take me out every evening to show me something or the other. Didi kept asking me why I went out every day. "If Baba hears about this, he will not be happy." But no one paid any heed to what she said. Her brother-in-law laughed and joked and teased me all the time. He used to spend a lot of time with me. In fact, he would keep talking to me and following me even when I was going off to sleep with his mother. Sometimes I would get quite fed up with him and he would reduce me to tears. But whenever that happened my Didi was always kind to me, and she would call me to her. Didi was round and plump—a bit like my father—and there were times when my cousins would tease her, call her "elephant" and try to make her angry. But even her brother-in-law had to stop teasing me when she told him off.

The days passed pleasantly in laughter and jokes with Didi's husband and her brother-in-law. I spent my time with her child, bathing him, talking to Didi about Ma and all our memories of old times spent in our home. Before I knew it, nearly a month had passed, and one day I heard that Baba, my new Ma, and my brother had come, and they were staying with my aunt. They'd come to have a bit of a break but also to fetch me. Didi sent a message that they must come to her home, that she considered our new Ma like our real mother so Baba should not hesitate to bring her with him. Two or three days after this message was sent, Baba brought everyone with him and came to Didi's home. Her husband and everyone at their home were extremely hospitable and they made them welcome. Of course many people whispered things about our new Ma, but the others decided there was no point in paying attention to such things and they just ignored them.

AFTER A WHILE AT DIDI'S PLACE, BABA TOOK ME BACK TO Aunt's house. Everyone was sorry to see me go—I'd been feeling sad ever since I had heard that he was coming to take us away, but there were tears even in Baba's eyes as we left. As she came out of the house, Didi was also crying, and she kept saying that whatever had to happen with her had already happened, but now her sister should not suffer the same fate.

When we got to Aunt's house, I heard that her daughter was to get married in some eight or ten days. This was the same girl to whom I had recounted the tale of the jackal and the farmer and then she had run out to meet the boy I'd seen at the window. I was happy to hear that she was to get married, but I was also a bit upset to hear that Baba had not taken enough time off from his workplace to be able to stay for the wedding, and that he also wanted to take me back with him—in fact, he'd come all the way to fetch me. My aunt realized what I was thinking and said to Baba, "If it's not possible for you to stay on, at least leave this poor motherless girl with me here." But Baba had made up his mind and refused to budge. Frustrated, my aunt suggested that at least he should meet my elder uncle before he left. Just when it seemed Baba might relent, our new mother interrupted and said they could not afford to delay. Having said that, they turned and left me and my brother in the room and went away.

Aunt was angry with Baba, and no sooner had he and my stepmother stepped out than she began to tell us all sorts of tales about him: things that we had not heard before and would not, even in our wildest imaginings, have thought. But they did not seem to be things said in anger. She told us that Baba had always been plump and round; that even as a child, he used to eat a lot, and because of this everyone called him Nadu Gopal, although his real name was Upendranath. He had not studied much but he had managed to get a good job. And this he got in the strangest way. One day he was working in the courtyard outside his home when an army van passed by. The people inside saw this healthy, well-built man and they called out to him and asked him to get into the van. Soon after that, people heard that he had joined the army. When my uncle heard this he was downcast: he felt he had lost his right arm, and did not know how he would manage. In those days everyone was afraid of army jobs because they were said to turn good men into rogues and this is why my grandmother was so angry when my father, his father, and one of their friends turned up at her house to see the woman who was to become our mother. But then, if it had not been fated that our mother, Ganga, would marry Upendranath, our father, how would it have happened?

Baba liked Ganga the moment he saw her. One day he turned up alone at her house to see her. He learned that she had gone to the village pond to bathe. When he managed to find the pond, he found that Ganga had finished her bath and was on her way back. She got really nervous when she saw him and quickly hid herself somewhere—she'd heard that military men were very violent and that they beat up women. Anyway, he did not manage to meet her that time, nor on several successive visits. Ganga's mother would get very irritated at his persistence. "This fellow just will not leave my daughter alone. He's determined to take her away," she said. And of course she was right.

Very soon things began moving, an auspicious time was fixed, and the marriage took place. Upendranath spent two or three months with his bride and then returned to his job. He wrote to his wife once a month, and he came home when my Didi was born. When he arrived, my grandmother put the child in his arms, saying: "She looks just like you." Baba started to laugh, at which my mother made a face and said sourly, "Look at the way he's laughing! He's so happy that he's got a daughter, and he's come running all this way. He's finally remembered that he has a home and a wife." My grandmother tried to tell Ma to be quiet: "He's come home after such a long time," she said, "and instead of making him welcome, all you can think of is reproaching him!"

But Baba said, "No, Ma, you be quiet. Let her say what she wants to."

"And why should I not speak?" retorted my mother. "This is the first time he's come back since we got married. If his job was so precious to him, why did he get married in the first place?" At this, everyone—my grandmother, my uncle, and everyone—burst out laughing. Baba was smiling and soon Ma also broke into a smile. My aunt teased Baba: "Brother, you'd better go and console your wife!"

Aunt would have told us more stories, but just then Baba came back. I think he had been getting our things together. He told my aunt that we would all go to our elder uncle's house and then carry on home from there. We then said good-bye to her and left.

WE SPENT A DAY AT MY UNCLE'S HOME. HE SEEMED QUITE worried about Didi, and said to my Baba, "You've sent her off to another home, but you have not bothered to keep track of whether she is happy or not. That poor girl, she must think she has no one at all: no mother, and a father who does not even seem to care about her anymore. At least go and see her once." Baba said he had just been to see her. At this, Uncle was quiet, then he pointed to me and said, "Don't make the same mistake with her. Make sure you check out the people you will marry her to." Baba looked at him, but I don't think he really heard what Uncle was saying.

That night, Uncle's elder daughter, my cousin, insisted that Baba tell us a story. Baba was a real storehouse of stories, so he began one for us, and before we knew it, half the night had gone. While we were listening, I kept thinking how lucky Uncle's daughters were! Five daughters, born one after the other as their parents each time tried for a boy, and yet Uncle had given them so much love. And he loved us the same way. I also liked my uncle very much. My grandfather had died while I was still a child, but I had heard people say that my uncle was tall and fair like him— just like my cousin, the long-awaited boy, who came after his five sisters.

When we said good-bye to Uncle, he seemed well and healthy, but just a few days later we heard that he had been taken ill. Baba and Ma went to see him, and when they returned they brought him back with them. One night Baba and Ma were talking and we heard them say that when they had gone to see Uncle, they had found him asleep. To Baba, he looked just like our grandfather at that moment and Baba began to cry when he saw him. Uncle woke up and said, "Don't cry, it's good you have come. I don't think I'm going to last much longer now. Somehow I have managed to marry off my one daughter but these little ones will now be your responsibility." Baba said, "Nothing is going to happen to you. I have come to take you home with me."

Baba brought Uncle back to Durgapur with him and took him to the company hospital to have him looked at. When he was a little better, Uncle's son, Shiv, came to our home to see his father. Uncle told him that he was feeling better but there was no guaranteeing how things would be in the future. Shiv then asked him to come back home, but Baba refused, saying that he would not let him go until he was satisfied that Uncle was fully recovered. Uncle would also have preferred that, but Shiv whispered something to him that seemed to change his mind. Uncle told Baba that since Shiv was insisting, it would be better for him to go. "Come on, son," he said to Shiv, "let's go."

Baba said, "Brother, since you are being treated here, wouldn't it be better to wait until your treatment is complete?" But Uncle was not willing to listen. Had it been anyone but Uncle, they, too, would not have wanted to stay with us, for it did not remain a secret for long that Ma was very upset over all the expense of Uncle's illness: she had talked about it loudly in the kitchen one day when Shiv was sitting outside and could hear everything.

Uncle left. One night, some days after this, I got up from bed to go to the bathroom. On my way out of the house, I saw Baba standing by himself in the dark. I asked him softly, "What's wrong, Baba?" He started to say something and then stopped. "Nothing. Nothing at all," he said, and he drew me gently toward him. I could see that there were tears in his eyes. Perhaps it was the dark that hid his tears from my stepmother, but she could not have mistaken who was standing with Baba outside. I couldn't understand why she did not come out, but just watched us through a crack in the door. After that night, Baba and Ma had many fights about me—so many that the whole house became full of tension, and I heard them say that the sooner I was married off, the better. Because of the tense atmosphere at home, Baba began to keep his distance from me, and I likewise avoided him. Did my stepmother really think that I, a twelve-year-old child, could have such an abnormal relationship with her father that his wife needed to be worried about it? To me, this was unimaginable, but that was precisely what my stepmother thought and that made things extremely difficult for me. I was so embarrassed by the whole thing that I found it difficult even to talk to the neighbors.

The escalating tension at home almost made me forget that not so long ago I had been a young girl who loved going to school. There were times when I felt that, like my own mother, I should also leave home and go away. But then, I would ask myself, where would I go? I had no place to call my own. I was consumed by such thoughts as the days somehow passed. Baba's attitude to me began to change visibly. I was no longer the apple of his eye, but more like a thorn in his flesh. The smallest things would irritate him, and somehow this just destroyed my confidence. I began to wonder and worry whether others too found me irritating.

I had stopped listening to the never-ending squabbles between Baba and Ma, but the lingering tension in the home affected me deeply. Every time I heard them complain about me, or about how they could get rid of me, I would go out of the house and cry. Then one day, when I could bear it no longer, I told Baba that I wanted to go to Aunt's house again. "You've only just been there," he said, "how can you go again? What will they think?" Baba and Ma joined forces against me, but I insisted. I wasn't going to give up that easily. I just dug in my heels, and in the end they had to agree. Perhaps Baba thought that this was the only way to ease the tension. I must have been right, because Baba then told me to go and tell Aunt everything about myself. "Perhaps she can do something for you," he said.

THE VERY NEXT DAY BABA BOUGHT ME A TICKET AND PUT me on the bus to my aunt's house. A few hours later I got off the bus and went straight to her son's shop, which was just by the bus stand. When I got there, I said to him, "Dada, I'm very hungry. Please give me something to eat." He looked a little worried when he saw me and said, "What's going on? Why are you here alone? Is everything all right at home?" He sounded really anxious. "Let me eat first," I said, "and then I'll tell you. I am really hungry." So he took me to a sweet shop where he sat me down on a bench and I ate my fill.

After that he took me home, and there I learned that the cousin to whom I had recounted the story of the jackal and the farmer, and who was to have been married, was still single. As she and I were talking, Aunt came in and she was shocked to see me. When she asked what I was doing there, I poured out the whole story about the constant bickering between Baba and my step-mother and the tension at home. She listened and her eyes filled with tears. "You did right to come," she told me, "and now you must stay here. In a couple of days some people are coming to see your Didi with a view to marriage, and your sister-in-law will have to cook for them. You can stay and help her."

That night my Didi and I talked long into the night. When I told her that the boy she was marrying was very good, she said, "How do you know?" I said that I'd overheard Aunt and Sandhya's mother talking and they were saying what a lovely pair they would make. At this, Didi blushed and said, "Okay, that's enough! Now go to sleep, it's late."

Now, if you go to bed late, you wake up late. But who was going to explain this to Aunt? She was in the habit of waking early and roasting the flat rice we call *mudi*, and it was our job to put together everything she needed for this. She would call us to wake up but we'd continue to sleep; then after several attempts, we'd get up, do her work, and go right back to bed. But she'd keep calling out to us while roasting the *mudi*, just to make sure that we didn't go back to sleep. If we didn't answer, she'd get angry and shout at us, saying, "These good-for-nothing girls have gone back to sleep again!" Then we'd quickly jump out of bed and go and do her bidding!

But even if she managed to wake us up, Aunt never told us what we were expected to do all day long. Didi was used to this, but I had spent a few years in school and I found it very difficult to hang around doing nothing. Visitors to Aunt's house would ask her about me if they saw me hanging around, and when she told them I was my father's daughter they found it difficult to believe that someone so young could have grown up so much. "Oh, Ma!" they'd cry, "that little girl? She's really grown up! She used to be such a child." I liked to hear them talk, particularly those who were from Murshidabad, because their way of speaking was very nice.

The people who came to see Didi were also from Murshid-abad and had the same sweet way of speaking, and perhaps because of that we were very hospitable to them. I helped to look after them. Aunt's daughter-in-law cooked for them, and it was my job to serve them tea and food. This I did enthusiastically, running around here and there in my dress, and I heard some people ask who this young and energetic girl was who was working so hard. Aunt immediately understood what lay behind that seemingly innocent question, and she told them that I was the daughter of a man who had a good job and it wasn't likely that he would give his daughter away to any old fellow.

After the visitors left, I realized how tired I was. I went outside the house, leaned against the wall, and sank to the ground with my legs spread in front of me. I liked sitting like that. I thought of all those people who had praised my work—what would they have said if they had known that ever since she was a small child, Baby had known little other than the hard drudgery of household chores?

Poor Baby! What else could one say of her? Imagine a childhood so brief, so ephemeral, that you could sit down and the whole thing would unravel in front of you in barely half an hour! And yet her childhood fascinates Baby. Perhaps everyone is fascinated by the things they've been deprived of, the things they long for. Baby remembers her childhood, she savors every moment of it, she licks it as a cow would her newborn calf, tasting every part. She remembers her Ma and Baba with their stories of Jammu and Kashmir where she was born, and how, when she arrived in the world, her eyes would not open easily because she'd come two months before her time. How, just a day before she was born, her father had left her mother in the hospital and gone to join the war, and there a bullet had hit him. And why would it not? With his wife lying in hospital, waiting to give birth, he could hardly have been expected to concentrate on anything else!

And there wasn't only Kashmir, but Dalhousie, too. Here, Baba would sometimes take the children for a walk in the evenings. The roads were so dark that they could not see a thing. They couldn't even hear the sound of approaching cars, and it wasn't until they saw their headlights that they were aware that there was a car on those dark roads. They'd walk along and come home frozen, where they would sit down in front of the one heater they had, crowding around it to try and get warm. Ma would tell them to make sure they put some mustard oil on their hands before going to bed, and then she'd do it for them and they'd fall asleep. When they awoke, it would still be dark and cold and it was difficult to know how late it was.

The house was quite high up, and from there they could see the mountains above them. From their house, the mountain roads looked like small and narrow strips and the cars going along them seemed like toy cars. Where would one find such a beautiful place? Baby remembered those days and wondered if Fate would ever allow her to go back there.

I know well what lay in store for Baby. Baba had told her to ask Aunt to make some "arrangement" for her, but after she had left, he must have talked to her stepmother about how difficult it was for them to manage without Baby around and they must have decided to get her to come back. Baby wondered what was so important that she had to be there. After all, there was nothing in the household tasks that someone else could not do. And then she remembered the one thing for which her presence was essential, and it made her smile. Baby's stepmother kept her head covered night and day, and she would never go out into the fields alone to relieve herself. Baba would not let her and it was Baby's job to accompany her into the fields! I'm embarrassed to even talk about it, but whatever it was, they had decided that they wanted to take Baby back and one day, they came to Aunt's house and did just that.

I MUST HAVE BEEN BACK FROM AUNT'S PLACE A COUPLE of months when, one day, my stepmother's brother came to our house and brought another man with him. My stepmother asked me to make tea for them and then came into the kitchen and asked me to serve the tea. I took the tea in and did as I was told, and my stepmother's brother, my uncle, asked me to sit down. I did so, and the man with him began to ask me questions. "What is your name? What is your father's name? Do you know how to sew? Can you cook? Can you read and write . . . ?" I was so nervous I could barely answer and I kept thinking, naively, that there must be some reason why he was asking me so many questions. At the time I could not have imagined that I would be married off to a man like him. I was a little over twelve years old and he was twenty-six!

After they'd eaten and drunk, Uncle took that man away. I went out to play and a friend of mine joined me. She was laughing and making fun of me. "So," she said, "they came to see you, didn't they?" I was taken aback. Then I laughed and said, "So what if they did? It will be a good thing to get married! At least I will get to have a feast." "Is that what you think?" she laughed, "that you yourself will get married and you will have a feast?" So I said, "Why not? Haven't you noticed how well people eat at weddings?" My friend gave me a funny look and burst out laughing. I didn't think this was out of the ordinary. After all, lots of people thought me a bit odd, because, apart from a few, I did not talk to many people and they did not talk to me. So often they used to think I was a bit strange.

A few days later the man who had come with my uncle returned with two others. At the time, I was playing outside dressed in my dress. My stepmother asked me to come inside. I thought, *Why have these people turned up again? What do they want now?* Then my brother pointed to one of them and said, "Look, this man will be our son-in-law." I turned to my stepmother and asked, "Ma, is this right? Will one of them be our son-in-law?"

At this my father, my stepmother, and my brother all burst out laughing. "You will always remain a *buddhu,* a fool," my father exclaimed, "I don't know what the future holds for you. When will you get some sense?" I felt that Baba was not happy with me.

I could never bear to see Baba unhappy. Whenever he was unhappy, whenever he shed tears, I would also weep. I remember one day my Didi beat up my brother and Baba stopped her, saying, "Don't beat him, child. Now you are the only one he has." He began to weep and my Didi and I had also burst into tears.

I suppose it was not wrong of Baba to call me foolish and mad in front of those people. I had not been able to say a word to them in response to all the questions that had been put to me. I felt too scared and tongue-tied. So Baba had answered them all—or rather, he had given them all sorts of evasive answers. When they asked about my brothers and sister, for example, Baba did not even mention the brother Ma took away with her when she left.

After they left, I thought of all the questions Baba had left unanswered. I thought, *If he had not even mentioned my little brother, why should he have told them about the scar he'd gotten on his forehead while playing?* One day, when I was still in class two, my brother had insisted on coming to school with me and Ma said, "Take him with you, if he wants to go." So I did. On the way we came across a water tap and he said he wanted a drink of water, so we went over to it. Suddenly, he slipped and fell and cut his forehead. He was bleeding profusely. I was so frightened I began to cry loudly. I covered his wound with my headscarf and we staggered home. Baba was not at home, but my mother quickly took my brother to the hospital. I did not even stop to wash my hands and rushed off to school as I was. But when everyone saw my bloody hands, they told the teacher and he sent me home. On the way back I met my Baba's friend Dhananjay Kaku, who knew what had happened—he must have met Ma on the way. Dhananjay Kaku was a good man—he was a potter by caste—and he always had a kind word for us. His home was close to our school and we often went there during break to watch his father at the potter's wheel—the movement of that wheel, and the way his father so deftly shaped the clay, fascinated us. We couldn't understand how, almost in the blink of an eye, a bit of mud could turn into a beautifully shaped pot.

The same visitors who had come to see me had also asked questions about my Didi. And all Baba had told them was that she was now married and at her in-laws' home. Had I not been so frightened to speak, imagine the things I would have told them! At her wedding, I'd brought my friends Dolly and Tutul over and we had spent our time eating and drinking until Dolly's grandfather came to fetch her and Tutul, who lived close by. Dolly's father was a friend of my father's and they often spent a lot of time together, so when he came Baba invited him in to share some sweets with him. There was also a band at Didi's wedding, and her husband had brought nearly seven hundred people with the *baraat*, the wedding party. We didn't expect so many people, but somehow we managed because Baba still had the pension he had gotten from his job and this money came in handy to feed all the wedding guests. Whatever was left he frittered away on drinking and on searching for my mother. He'd also had some jewelry made for Didi, and I remember that she had asked him why he was spending so much money. "How will my sister feel if you spend all your money on me?" she had asked. "Why not get some made for her as well?" In fact, she told him that if he did not do so, she wouldn't wear any jewelry herself. So he made some small things for me, too—little earrings, and things like that. And Didi made me put them on—everyone thought I looked so beautiful!

One day, shortly after Didi's wedding, I'd gone to visit my aunt and while combing my hair there, one of my earrings got caught in my hair and broke. My stepmother asked me to give her all my ornaments, saying she would have them properly made again, so I handed them over. For a long time after that there was no sign of them at all. No one said a word, and even when I asked about them there was no response. But soon afterward I noticed my stepmother was wearing new earrings ... while the disappearance of my jewels still remained a mystery. If I ever asked about my things I was told they were at the repair shop, and after that I heard no more about them.

My stepmother and my father had had a love marriage, and that, too, in a Kali temple! Baba and she both drank. At first they would drink when we were not around, but as time passed, they lost that discretion and were often drunk and boisterous in front of us. We did not like this, but no matter what we said to try and embarrass them, it made no difference. They just drank if they wished to, and heard what they wanted to hear. Strangely, we were the ones who ended up feeling ashamed, and we'd then make ourselves scarce and get out of their way! We were at a loss to understand what we could do. Baba and my stepmother continued to be in love even after their marriage. Every day at mealtimes, they would argue: if one did not eat, the other refused to do so, too. They had special names for each other. She would say, "Mana, you eat first." And he would say, "No, Rani, *you* eat first." And if sometimes Baba lost his temper and refused to eat, he'd stomp off to work and then she would refuse to eat as well.

All this went on, and before I knew it I was twelve years and eleven months old. One day I saw Baba and my maternal aunt coming back from the bazaar with bags full of vegetables. They gave the bags to me to empty out and I did that carefully. As I came out, I noticed a suitcase lying nearby. I asked Baba about it and he told me it had things for my wedding. My stepmother and aunt opened the suitcase and showed me what was inside. I was so happy to see all those wonderful things! The next day, Baba brought me a new quilt, a mattress, and a pillow and I was beside myself with joy! Outside the house, some people had put up a sort of awning, and beneath it sat a large *chulah* mounted on bricks. The whole neighborhood was filled with music. I was watching all this and playing with the children outside when my aunt called me inside and asked me to be seated on a *pidi*. My stepmother then began to smear turmeric paste on my body, and then others came and joined in. I was told that I could not eat that day, that I had to fast. I was surprised: as far as I knew, fasts were kept on religious days, but there was no festival then . . .

Now, when she thinks back, Baby wonders how she spent that day of sorrow in such merriment. Little did Baby know that this was the beginning of her days of grief and pain, little did she know what the future held for her. On the seventeenth day, a Wednesday in the month of Agrahayan, Baby was married.

ON WEDNESDAY NIGHT, I WAS MARRIED. BUT I SPENT THAT entire night chatting with my friends, some local girls and an older woman from the area. The next day was a Thursday, and Ma said she would not send me away on such an inauspicious day. Before I knew it, the day became like every other and I quickly lost myself in household tasks. Every now and again, I'd sing and jump about and play. There were no tears in anyone's eyes that day: not in my mother's, not in mine. I was carefree and happy. And I laughed a lot that day. In the afternoon, after I'd bathed, I got dressed. I pulled out a dress and when my aunt saw me she laughed and said, "No, no, not that! You should wear a sari." I did not know how to—my wedding day was the first time I'd actually worn one. So I asked my aunt if she could help me to tie it, and so she did.

On Friday, one of the women from the neighborhood came and helped me dress. She'd done that for me and my husband on the wedding day, too. Then a taxi was called and my husband and I were seated inside. My mother's brother and sister and my own brother also sat with us. I had no idea where we were going or why. As we sat down, my aunt came up to me and put a handful of rice and dal in my *aanchal* and whispered to me that I should give these to my mother, and say: "Ma, with these I pay you back for all the days you have fed and clothed me, and looked after me." I did as she asked, but I noticed that as I said this, Baba began to cry. I looked at him and I also burst into tears. At this, he cried even harder. With tears running down his face, he clutched my husband's hand and said, "Son, I've given you my daughter: now it's up to you to look after her. She's a motherless child."

The taxi started off. My husband's home was not far from ours—the bus fare was only three rupees. When the taxi pulled up a woman from the neighborhood came up and took my hand to help me out. She then led me into my new home. People crowded around, offering me sweets, urging me to eat, but I was so terrified, I could not even open my mouth! Even when my uncle and aunt pressed me to eat, I refused. All I could do was to stare at all the people collected there.

Later, in the afternoon, one of the women came and dressed me up, sprinkling fistfuls of vermilion powder on my head. I just sat quietly in a corner. People had gathered there to get a glimpse of the new bride, and I had covered my hair according to my aunt's instructions. They came to see me and they gave me money and utensils or other gifts. Then they sat down to eat. When they'd finished, someone from outside called for the new bride to be sent out. A woman caught hold of my hand and pulled me outside to where everyone was sitting. She handed me a *handi* full of sweets and said, "Now take this and serve everyone. Put two pieces on everyone's *pattal* leaf." I was so nervous and my hands were shaking so much that every time I put a piece on someone's plate it would end up somewhere else! I didn't know what to do, whether to make sure my head was covered because the *pallu* kept slipping off, or to serve the sweets.

All the time my aunt's instructions to keep my head covered were buzzing around in my head. Frustrated, I angrily put the *handi* down and started to set my sari *pallu* right on my head when everyone started to laugh. I was mortified. I wished the ground would open and just swallow me up! I left the *handi* right there and fled into the house, where I cried and cried. Meanwhile people started to tease my husband. "So, Shankar," they said to him, "you've brought home a mere child! What are you going to do with such a young wife?" Then the woman who had taken me out came back and again took me by the hand, saying, "Come along, today is the *bahu bhaat*. The new bahu has to serve everyone." So I went out again and this time, somehow, I managed to serve everyone. I felt as if every part of me was trembling as I did this. When everyone had finished eating, it was my husband's turn. And then, when he had finished, my aunt said I should eat from his plate.

I began to insist that I wanted to eat with her and my uncle, but my uncle scolded me, saying, "We're not going to be here forever, you know. You're the one who has to be here. Just be quiet and eat." And as soon as they finished eating, my uncle, aunt, and my brother left.

Now I was alone with my husband. I kept looking at him and wondering what he would do now, but he did not utter a word. I kept watching him quietly. For a little while, he did this and that, all sorts of little chores in the room, then he spread a mat on the *chowki* and indicated to me that I should sleep there. I lay down on the *chowki* and fell asleep immediately. In the night, I woke up with a start and found him lying next to me! I sat up, frightened, then I moved away and spread a small mat on the floor and went to sleep there.

In the morning when I woke up, I noticed that my husband's house was by a *pukka* road, and it had a tiled roof. The rent for the house was one hundred rupees—this I found out from the woman who had helped me out of the taxi. She was called Sandhya. My husband addressed her husband as Dada, elder brother. Sandhya called me "sister" and I referred to her as Didi, elder sister. They lived across the road from us. They had a tap in their house from where I would get water. We even had to go there to use the toilet, since we didn't have one in our own home. Sandhya-di told me I should look upon her husband as my elder brother-in-law. "Your husband calls him Dada," she said, "and whenever you are in his presence, you should cover your head." Her husband had a lot of regard for me and whenever I was around someplace, he would quickly move away. He had a machine for cutting fodder, which he would buy in the market, cut at home, and then sell. Talking to Sandhya-di, watching *chara* being cut, the days passed well enough, but no sooner would evening come than I would be filled with fear and dread. My heart would start beating frantically. I used to sleep on the same mat as my husband, but I'd turn my head the other way. Three or four days passed like this and then, suddenly, one night, he caught hold of me and pulled me roughly toward him. He put his hand on my breast and told me in a gentle voice that he did not like living like this and he no longer wanted to do so. And so saying, he began to press his body against mine. I started to cry out in fear. But then, I thought, what's the point? I'll just wake everyone by shouting like this, so I shut my eyes and my mouth tightly and let him do what he wanted. I just endured everything.

The next morning when I went to see Sandhya-di, she took one look at my face and asked me what was wrong. "What happened?" she said. After a short while, I told her I wanted to go back to my father's home. Then I came back home and began to prepare the fire to cook. It was then that I looked up and saw my brother walking down the road toward our house. The moment he stepped through the door I announced, "I'm coming back with you."

"Why? Where's brother-in-law?"

I told him he was inside, so my brother went into the room and asked my husband, "Whatever's the matter, brother-in-law? Why is Baby so upset?"

Shankar laughed and said, "Nothing's the matter. Your sister still thinks she's a little girl." When he heard this, my brother just turned around and went home alone. When he got there, Baba asked him, "You'd gone to see your Didi, hadn't you?" And he said, "Yes, and she's very unhappy. She burst into tears when she saw me."

Ma and Baba were so disturbed that they didn't waste a moment. The very same day they rushed to our house. Baba asked Shankar, "I heard Baby was crying, son. What happened?" But Shankar did not say anything. I said, "Baba, I don't want to stay here."

"All right," he replied. "Why don't both of you come back with us for a while?" And so we went back with them. As the new son-in-law, my husband was given a lot of importance in Baba's house. All sorts of delicious dishes were prepared for him. And as for me, everyone kept explaining that I must understand that I wasn't a child anymore.

Two days passed and it was time to return. But I began to throw tantrums again, saying I wouldn't go back. Ma got angry with me. Then I began to think: perhaps it was better to be in my

own house after all. In Baba's house I still had to do all the work
and got no appreciation at all. At least my husband's house wasn't
like that. There, I could work as I wished, when I wished, and
there was nobody getting at me all the time. I could cook what I
wanted, when I wanted, and if I needed anything for the house, I
simply asked him and he would bring it. Whenever I had a little
free time, I went across to Sandhya-di's. She had three sons and
sometimes, watching them play, I was sorely tempted to join in.
There were times when I did—I'd become the old Baby then, and
we'd laugh and play and I'd join in their fun and games. Sandhya-
di and her husband watched us, and they often laughed when
they saw me like this. I could never understand why they found
this so amusing. When I asked, Sandhya-di said to me, "We're
laughing because you are still such a child." I felt very embarrassed
when I heard this—it was true, I thought. I'm no longer a child.
I'm a woman now, and I haven't seen any women jumping and
playing like this.

About two months after I'd come back from Baba's house, I
suddenly began to feel quite ill. I wanted to throw up, and this
feeling persisted for a few days. I couldn't eat properly: nothing
would stay down. One day Sandhya-di asked me whether I'd
had my period that month. I told her that I'd only had it once
since my marriage, so she talked to my husband and told him he
should take me for a checkup. But he didn't listen to her, so she
decided to take me herself and we went together to the govern-
ment hospital. We ran from one person to another, and in the end
we learned that the examination for pregnancies was only done
on Fridays and Tuesdays. That day we came back, frustrated, and
on Friday, we went again. Once there, I had to fill in a form, and
then when my name was announced, I went in to be examined by
a lady doctor. I stood in front of her like a deaf-mute. She asked
me many things, but no words came out of my mouth. Then she

asked if anyone had come with me and I told her my Didi had, so she asked me to call her in.

She asked Sandhya-di a lot of questions about me and then she turned to me and told me to lie down on the bed. I did as she asked and then she began to examine me. She put her hand between my legs and felt around inside. Then she turned to Sandhya-di and announced: "She is pregnant." I sat up with a start, speechless with fear, but Sandhya-di only laughed. When we got home I could find nothing to say to my husband, but Sandhya-di said to him, "Listen, it's as I thought. What I was imagining has happened."

"What's happened?" he asked.

"Well, the first thing you should do is to distribute sweets to everyone," she said. Then she told him and her husband what the doctor had said. I felt from their laughter that they were all happy. Two days later, when Baba and Ma came to see me, Sandhya-di gave them the news as well. Ma laughingly said to Baba, "Did you hear that? We're going to have a small visitor in the house!" But I thought Baba did not look too happy. Two days later, when they were going back to their home, I overheard Baba talking to Ma. "Rani," he said, "having a child at such a young age, won't that be dangerous?" My stepmother had no children of her own, but she knew things from here and there and she reassured him, "No, no. She'll be fine."

After Baba and Ma left, I went to fetch water. Suddenly I saw Sandhya-di's husband in front of me. I did not take any notice until I heard Sandhya-di calling out to me and that's when I realized my mistake. I'd forgotten to cover my head! She was signaling to me frantically, pointing to him and then to my head, and I quickly put my pot down and covered my head. Just then I saw a number of Baba's friends coming down that road—they were on their way to work. It's a good thing my head was covered, because if they had recognized me they would have started up on the same things they used to say every day: "Look, there's Halder-da's daughter!" one would say. Another would ask his friend in surprise, "So this is where Halder has got his daughter married off?" And another would chip in: "Didn't he check out anything at all? Why did he do this?"

Whenever I saw them coming down the road I would run into the house and hide. I was terribly ashamed. Sometimes they would call out to me and say, "Hey, girl. So this is where you live, eh?" But I would not answer. I'd just turn my face away and stay silent. I don't know what effect these things had on Baba, but it was true that he hardly visited me these days. He took the same route to go to work but often when he saw me he pretended not to, and would look away. Even if he was with a friend or someone else and that person said, "Look, isn't that your daughter?" he still would not acknowledge me. At such times, I understood that he was doing this deliberately, and it would upset me a lot. Sometimes I would go home and weep: sometimes I would go and talk to Sandhya-di. But gradually I began to realize that Baba now wanted to be free of me: he had sent me away and that was that. He no longer wanted to be burdened with my problems.

There was another reason why I often fled to Sandhya-di's house. Our home was between a large house and a restaurant, at the edge of a road. I felt ashamed to be living in this little hut we called home. When my husband was not home, all sorts of people walking by on the road would peer into the house, so I felt much better when I was at her house. One day, as we were chatting about this and that, I said to her, "Sandhya-di, why don't we go to see a film?" Normally, her husband did not allow her to leave the home but this time round, he agreed because I was there, and he used to treat me like his own daughter. He gave her a little money and said, "Go ahead, go to the cinema." Now it was my turn to ask my husband—but he never really talked to me. In the morning, when we woke, I would make him tea and some *roti* and *sabzi*, and he'd eat and then leave for work. In the afternoon, he'd return and go straight to the tap outside, have a wash, then come back and lie down. Even if I asked him anything, he would not reply. Whether he was in the house or not didn't seem to make much difference: even when he was, it was as though he were absent. When I mentioned to him that Sandhya-di and I wanted go to the cinema, he merely laughed and said nothing. But I kept on at him and finally he gave me some money. I thought then that if it were up to him, he would never take me anywhere nor let me go anywhere myself. When I came back from the cinema he was sitting with his face puffed up in anger. He would not talk to me properly and when I put his food in front of him, he just gulped it down and moved away. Given his behavior, I had little hope that he would bother to come to the hospital with me when my time came.

My stomach was growing bigger by the day and I was a little concerned. When I told Sandhya-di, she said I should get Shankar to take me to the hospital. But I told her it was no use: he would not take me. In the end, when no one was willing to come with me yet everyone kept saying that I should show myself to the doctor, I decided one day to go by myself, alone. First no one would believe I was with child, but after the examination, when they realized I was seven months pregnant, the nurse gave me an injection. Then I came home. I was a little less worried now, because I had understood that what was happening to me was the same thing that happened to every girl.

Now people began to say to my father, Halder-da, your daughter is seven months pregnant, you have to feed her the *sadh*. I had no idea what *sadh* was or how it should be eaten, but I was happy because Baba and Ma came to fetch us to their home and they went to the market and bought vegetables, meat, fish, and all sorts of nice things. They also bought me a sari and a blouse. On that occasion Ma's sister, whom we called Badi-ma, and her three daughters also came. Badi-ma cooked all the food and Ma prepared the *kheer*. Then, as they talked, Ma put some *kheer* in a bowl and then looked around for a basket to cover it with. She took the vegetable basket and turned the vegetables out on the floor, covering the *kheer* with the upturned basket.

Ma told Baba that he should go and bathe but he said, "First let us finish with Baby and then we will see." Ma put seven types of vegetables and *kheer* into a *thali* and then sent me off to wear the sari. I came back dressed in the sari and bent to touch Baba's feet, but as I did so, he recoiled. Shocked, I stood up. Baba said, looking at Ma, "If a girl is pregnant, it is not good to receive her greetings. You don't know whether she is carrying a snake or a frog or god in her womb." When she heard this, Badi-ma also refused to accept my greetings and she said, "Go and sit down, today you will eat first and all of us will eat afterward." As I sat down to eat, Ma came and uncovered the *kheer* to see if it had curdled or not. If it curdles it is believed that the child will be a girl and if it does not, it is assumed the child will be a boy. The *kheer* had not curdled and Ma was overjoyed. "It will be a boy! It will be a boy," she cried to Baba. Baba was also very happy, and all the neighbors milling around sounded overjoyed at the prospect of a son.

After I had eaten, Baba, Ma, Badi-ma, and her daughters sat down to eat. Baba said to Badi-ma, "Didi, I am very frightened. I hope it will not be dangerous to bring a child into the world at a time like this." Badi-ma rubbished this, saying, "Don't be silly, nothing will happen." In the midst of all these celebrations, my husband suddenly decided that he wanted to go home. What a strange thing to do! Everyone tried to dissuade him: "Let it be for today," they said, "She's just had the *sadh*, how can you take her home on the same day? She can't leave today." He finally agreed, but said that he would go anyway. "You can bring her home later," he told them. He was odd, my husband. He had no social graces and did not know how to talk to his elders or how to offer them respect, and if I ever told him that he should try to be respectful, he would just glower at me.

The next day Badi-ma and Baba took me back to my home. On the way Badi-ma explained to me that I should not step out of the house in the evenings, and if I had to do so, it should be in my husband's company. After they left, I went into the house. The filthy state of the place made me want to turn right round and run back. I'd only been away a day and the house was a real mess. My husband was also very unclean personally. He never cleaned his teeth or washed his face properly. I hated having to eat from his used plate. If I told him to clean his teeth properly, he would ignore me. And somehow he managed to mess up that tiny house so easily. He would never lift up the broom to sweep, and if I was out for a few days, all the dishes and utensils would remain piled up in a dirty heap, waiting to be washed. Often I had no desire to enter the house but forced myself to do so, telling myself that it was only by being a man that you could have such privileges. And it was no use trying to say anything to this man, since my words fell on deaf ears.

One day, when I was eight months pregnant and could stand this no more, I went to Baba's house. I had imagined I would get some peace there, but the moment I arrived I heard that my mother's brother was very sick: he had been diagnosed with tuberculosis. As soon as they heard this, my Ma began to cry and Grandmother began to shout abuses, cursing her, as if this were all her fault. Baba took Uncle to see the best possible doctors in Dur-

gapur and my aunt would bring the money from her own home
to pay for whatever medicines they prescribed.

My aunt was my uncle's second wife. Despite many years of
being married, she had no children of her own. His first wife went
away one day to visit her parents and when she did not come back
for a long time, my uncle took a second wife. His first wife left
behind a young daughter who was with her father for a while
but then, when she insisted that she wanted to go back to her
mother, my aunt took her back and left her there. My uncle's
health began to decline soon after that, which is why Dadi-ma
was cursing her.

That night, my brother and I finished our meal and went to
sleep. Ma and Baba always fed us first before they ate themselves.
I was nodding off when I heard Baba say to Ma, "Call Baby and
ask her to come and eat a little more." Ma said, "Why don't you
call her yourself?" He called out to me and I told him I was not
hungry, but still he insisted: "Come, child, come and sit with me
for a while." Whenever I went to Baba's house, it was always like
that. Some days they would be so kind to me, they would treat me
really well, and feed me all kinds of good things. If Baba saw that
I was hesitating to eat, he would leave a little food in his plate and
tell me to eat it whenever I felt hungry. Ma did not lag behind, either; whatever she cooked, she would put aside a little for me.
One day as I sat down to eat, Ma asked me if my husband ever
brought fish or meat home. I said he did but very rarely. At this,
Ma called him a miser and put an extra piece of fish on my plate,
saying, "Here, eat this. And if you are still hungry, just let me
know." It was odd. On the one hand they looked after me and fed
me with such love and care, but on the other, they quarreled about
me over all sorts of minor matters. When Ma was angry she had
no real control over her tongue and she would say all sorts of

things. Finally, when I could bear it no more, I said: "Ma, I have no desire to eat fish or meat, and if my presence is causing you such problems, I had better just go." I started to put my things together to leave but she stopped me, saying, "Don't go just now. If you must go, at least wait till the afternoon."

"No, I won't stay on, and I won't come back ever, since my presence causes such problems for you and Baba."

"But it's your Baba who causes the problems."

"Baba is a good person, you're a good person, everyone is good, but as soon as I arrive, you start bickering, and I can't bear to see this." I made as if to go and she again stopped me. "At least wait to say good-bye to your Baba before you leave."

"Where is he?" I asked.

"He has gone up to the pond. Let him come back and then you can leave."

"But I'll be late, I have to get back and see to the cooking and everything . . ." The words were barely out of my mouth when I saw Baba coming back. Ma said to him, "Look, she's all ready to go back! Please tell her to at least eat before she leaves."

"If your mother is asking you to wait, why don't you do so for a while?" Baba asked me.

I said, "What? And listen to that squabbling again? I can't bear this tension between the two of you because of me. God knows why it happens, but I must leave."

I would have said more, but just then my cousin came running and cried out to Ma that her brother had died. Ma began to cry, and Grandmother, who was there, fainted. Baba did not know what to do or who to look after. He took Ma with him and went quickly to her brother's house. I was left at home with Grandmother. Many of the neighbors came along to comfort her. I sat her down and sprinkled her forehead with water, but she was inconsolable, and kept sobbing.

When Ma and Baba got to Uncle's home, they found his body laid out in front of the house. Ma sat down at his feet and began to cry. My aunt's grief was different. Everyone around had been so unkind to her because she had not borne any children and she, too, no longer had any real interest in my uncle. The neighbors got everything ready to take Uncle away. Ma was sent to fetch Grandmother so she could look at her son's face one last time. But then everyone began to say that she shouldn't be taken to see him, that she would not be able to stand to see him like that, and so Ma showed her his face from quite far away and then took her into the house.

Uncle had no son, so his last rites had to be performed by Grandmother's younger son. He had had his head shaved for this. On the *satkarya* day, they all went and left me at home—I had not left until then because Baba had held me back, saying he would not be able to manage two distraught and grief-stricken women on his own.

The moment the rituals were over, I set off for home. When I got there, I found the house was locked. I went to Sandhya-di's. When she saw me she exclaimed, "*Arre*, you're back so soon? We were just talking about you. We thought you'd finish everything and then come back."

"Do you think anyone can survive that daily bickering?" I replied. "I was going to come back much earlier but because my uncle died, I had to stay on. Do you know why my house is locked up? How will I get in?"

"There's nothing you can do. Just wait here till Shankar comes back."

"Can you not ask Bhagirath to take a look? My husband may still be at the decorator's shop." So Sandhya-di sent her son off to find him.

Sandhya-di was Bengali and her husband Bihari, so she

would speak to her children and her husband in Bihari, but would talk to me in Bengali. In a short while, Bhagirath came back with the key. He said he'd found my husband at the shop and when he told him that I had returned, my husband just gave him the key and sent him straight back. I took the key and went home. When I opened the door, the sight that assailed me made my head spin: the house was filthy, with dust and mud everywhere; the kitchen was full of mouse holes where they had dug up the earthen floor and nested; all the utensils were lying in a heap, soiled from being used and caked with dried-up food. It was so terrible that I felt deeply ashamed. I could not bear it, and I ran to Sandhya-di's house and began beating my head on the wall. When she asked me what was wrong I said to her, "Didi, just come and take a look at the state of the house."

"I know what it is like," she said, "I don't need to see for myself. This is what happens when there is no woman in the house." After a while she added, "I noticed that often there were days when he would not even bathe, and he'd cook in the same dirty utensils and eat."

"But why should it need a woman around for a place to stay clean? A man should at least keep the place where he cooks and eats clean."

Sometimes Grandmother would visit me. One day when she came, I said to her, "Look, just look at what a state my home is in."

"My dear child," she said to me, "everything is in your hands. You need to sit him down and explain to him."

"I've tried! But he just won't listen to anything I say. If I so much as open my mouth, he jumps down my throat! I don't know what to do."

Sometimes when I felt very alone in the house and got fed up with staying inside, I would go out, cross the road, and watch the children playing. I wanted so badly to go and play with them. One day, I was standing outside the house watching the children play *gulli danda*. Suddenly the *gulli* flew through the air and landed at my feet. I thought I would pick it up and throw it back to the children, but the moment I touched it—I don't know what happened to me—instead of throwing it back, I picked it up and ran into the field where they were playing and joined in. I lost track of the time, and I would have gone on playing with them but one of them caught hold of my hand and said, "Didi, that lady over there is calling you." I looked and saw that some women standing by my house were watching me, and one of them, whom I called Aunt, was calling out to me. When I got to her, she chided me: "What on earth do you think you're doing? What if you hurt your stomach? Look at the size of you! You can hardly walk and you think nothing of rushing off into the field to play! Get back inside at once!"

Shamefacedly, I ran into the house. Everyone in the neighborhood began to make fun of me, especially the young boys and girls, who said, "Look at the new bride! She can hardly move and she is playing *gulli danda*!" When I heard this, I couldn't help but laugh.

When I was this happy, my husband's house did not seem so bad. In Baba's home I had found it so difficult because of the continuous tension, but here there were only two people and one of them was hardly ever home. He would fight and go away, and then to console myself I would watch the children play, or go to visit Sandhya-di, who was always ready to give me support. It was Sandhya-di who had told my husband to give me whatever I wanted to eat. That way, she told them, my child's mouth wouldn't water unduly. And I, fool that I was, believed he would do as she said and I began to dream about what I would ask him for. I decided that when the time came, I would demand some *chop mudi*. Just thinking of this made me happy; I truly believed he would do as I said, and so I waited for the day to end and the right moment to come. As the hours passed, my anticipation increased and so did my happiness. Then I suddenly remembered that he would not be home in the evening, so I thought, *Why don't I ask him now?* But how could I? We hardly spoke to each other . . . I told myself, it has to be done, let me try once and see what happens. So I went into the kitchen. He was sitting there on a stool, and I kept hovering about. He was looking at me and I at him. Then I told myself that the *chop mudi* would not come by itself, so I plucked up courage and asked him, with a smile, to give me some money. I had to say it two or three times, but finally he pulled some money out of his *lungi* and sort of threw it at me rather reluctantly and left.

My husband never gave any money to me. I had to ask him for each and every little thing I needed. He would decide whether he wanted to give me money or not. All kinds of vendors would come into our neighborhood to sell things, and I felt very bad when I saw all the other girls buying from them. Even when there was shopping to be done at the market, he would go himself. Finally, when I could not stand being without money at all, I thought up a plan. When I sat down to cook, I would put aside a fistful of rice every day. After several days when I saw him going out of the house with a bag, I asked if he was going to buy rice, and when he answered yes, I said to him, "I have some rice, would you like to buy that?" He laughed and said, "Show it to me, how many days will it last?"

"Oh, two or three days."

At this, he put the bag down and, without saying anything to me, went off to work. Foolishly, I had thought I would earn a few rupees this way. Perhaps it would have been better if I hadn't said anything at all.

The next morning he was drinking tea when I said to him, "Please bring some rice, otherwise I will not be able to cook."

"But you said you had enough for two or three days," he said.

"If you pay me, I will cook that rice." He started to laugh but he did not say anything.

"Don't you think I need money for some small expenses?" I said. "You will never buy anything for me, and if you don't give me at least some money, how do you expect me to manage? I can't buy anything if I want to! Everyone here buys something or the other now and again, but what about me? I just stand and watch."

"Here, take this," he said, and handed me ten rupees.

"Two, three kilos of rice for just ten rupees? I will not give you my rice for this pittance."

He started to laugh so I said, "Don't laugh. I have saved this by eating a little less every day, but if this is all you're going to give me then I will not save rice like this anymore."

"Of course, you don't get anything to eat here! I suppose you think it's your father who feeds you, I don't give you anything at all."

"What do you give me," I asked, "other than a few morsels to eat? Do you think I have no desires at all in my life? Every morning you give me the same handful of rice and vegetables, and it never occurs to you how I will make do with so little. You eat your fill and get up, without once asking me if I have eaten or not, whether my stomach is full or not." But all this had no effect on him.

I thought I should say more, but just then Ma arrived. We made desultory conversation and then she asked me if I had been to the hospital. When I told her I hadn't and she realized that my pregnancy was nearly full-term, she said, "Come on, come along with me. We'd better make arrangements for when the child arrives." My husband listened to all this and did not say a word even as I got my things ready. I left with Ma.

The first two or three days in Ma and Baba's house were pleasant enough, and then their bickering began again. This time round, things seemed much worse and then one day, Baba really lost his temper. He said to Ma, "You're a fine one, you brought the girl here promising her peace and quiet and now that she is here, you fight with her about every little thing." Ma muttered something in reply, I could not make out what it was, and Baba began to shake with anger. He was so furious that he began to beat her. He was shouting at her and she at him. I tried hard to get them to calm down, but they were in no mood to listen. Then my temper began to rise. I thought, *Are these people unable to spend even one day in peace?* "I made a mistake in coming here," I said to Ma. "If my coming causes you such trouble, I don't know why you asked me to come at all. You should have just left me there. Oh, God, what have I done to deserve this, is there no peace for me anywhere?" As I said this, I began to beat my head.

Baba rushed toward me—perhaps he was afraid that I might hurt myself—and made as if to pick me up. Then he looked at Ma and held back. Standing there, he said, "Don't cry, child, please don't cry." This made me even angrier than ever, and I began to wail even more loudly. Then he turned to Ma: "Rani, stop her, otherwise she will die. Oh, God," he cried, "what have I done? What has happened to my daughter?"

He called out to a neighbor, "Brother, look at my daughter. Why is she doing this? What has come over her?" The neighbor came and stood a little way away, calling across, "Baby? What's wrong?" By this time my temper had skyrocketed and I was in a rage. In the heat of my fury, I was blind to the fact that my clothes were half undone. The blood was pounding in my head. I picked up a large *hansia* and held it up. "Don't come near me," I threatened. "If anyone comes close I will chop them up with this."

At this, Baba fell at my feet and began crying. "Calm down, child. Calm down, I beg you." My grandmother came up behind me and said, "Will you put that down or not?" As she said this, she gently pulled it out of my hands and let it slide down, and along with it I fell to the ground with a thud. Baba then rose up and said to Ma, "Rani, put some balm on her forehead." While she did this, Baba gently told me to sit up. I did as I was told and set my clothes right. "I'll leave tomorrow morning," I said.

"All right, go if you must, but right now, just calm down." Then, weeping, he said, "I'm so sorry, every time you come there is trouble in the house. I'm so sorry I have not been able to give you even a bit of peace. I earn so much and yet I am not able to feed you properly. What kind of father am I? Go away, child, this is no place for you. You will not be able to live here. Take whatever you have, whatever is your due, and leave."

That night I went to bed hungry. It was quite late at night when Ma woke Baba and asked him to eat. Baba called out to me and said, "Come, child, come and eat something."

"I don't feel like it," I answered, "I'm not hungry." But both of them came and took hold of my hands, pulled me up, and gave me food. In the morning, my grandmother took me home. When we arrived, she went to meet my maternal aunt and then returned.

Three days after this, my pains started. That morning Baba had sent my brother to the market and had told him to look in on me on the way back. When he came and found me lying down he asked what the matter was. I told him I wasn't feeling well. My husband was also there at the time. He told my brother, "Your mother was quick to take her away, but she wasn't able to keep her there for long."

"Didi was right to come away," my brother said. "That place is not good for her. I'm also going to leave soon."

"But where will you go?" I asked him.

"Do you think anyone can live there?" he said. "Why did your mother take her away then?" my husband interrupted. "Just to show how much she loves her, right?"

I could feel the pain getting worse. My brother must have told Baba about my state, for that very day he and Ma came to see me. Baba told my husband that he thought I should be taken to the hospital straightaway. Shankar rounded on him: "So when you took her away saying you would see what happened, why did you not keep her there? Why have you sent her back?"

"Her place is here, this is her lot . . ." was all Baba said in reply, and then he and Ma left.

During this time, Sandhya-di often came to see me. One day she said to my husband, "Shankar, she's been in pain for two days now, and nothing is happening. Why don't you go and call the midwife?" He didn't say yes or no but when Sandhya-di insisted, he finally went and called the *dai*. The moment she arrived, she sent everyone out of the room, and then she examined me just as the hospital doctor had done some time ago. Then she massaged my stomach and said, "There's still two or three days before the child is ready to come, but you need to rest till then. You can get up, though." I began to tremble with fear. She set my clothes right and then told me that if I had made a knot in any of my clothes or in a rope, I should undo it. Then she made me open the lids of all the spice boxes, and then she put them back on herself. I began to weep. *What on earth have I let myself in for?* I thought. The *dai* sat with me for a while, and then she called Sandhya-di in and left.

Five days later I was still in pain and nothing had happened. The pain was intermittent but when it came, I had no idea what to do. When it eased off, I wanted to get up, to go out for a walk, or to go and talk to everyone. During the day, Sandhya-di looked after me and offered me all sorts of things to eat. She forced me to drink hot milk, hot tea, and hot water in the belief that if I did not eat anything, the child would have difficulty being born. At night I slept alone and when the pain swept over me, I would sometimes scream in agony, but it made not a jot of difference to my husband, who slept through it all. On the sixth day, the *dai-ma* came again and gave me a massage. She examined me again, and said I still had to give it more time. My pain was increasing slowly and along with that, my tears and screams were also more frequent. That day, the *dai-ma* spent the whole day with me. I had not eaten or slept properly for the last six days and I was sure I was going to die.

When six days had passed and nothing had happened, Sandhya-di began to worry. She called my husband and said, "Shankar, what is this you are doing? This has been going on so long, and yet you have made no arrangements at all. Go, take her to the hospital." That night, around nine, Sandhya-di and her husband got ready to come with me, my husband, and the *dai-ma* to the hospital. When Sandhya-di put out her hand to support me, I began to cry. I felt so weak I could hardly walk. But everyone persuaded me that I would have to manage somehow, and then they helped me into a truck that was standing there. We all climbed in and set off for the hospital. Once I was admitted, they all got back into the truck and left.

IN THE HOSPITAL I—A CHILD, NOT EVEN FOURTEEN YEARS old—I, Baby, lay there alone crying and screaming. When the other patients began complaining, Baby was moved to another room, where she was put on a table and her arms and legs were tied. An *ayah* and a nurse came now and again to look at her.

When she began to scream louder, the *ayah* called a doctor. The doctor put her on a saline drip and pronounced that she was in a bad state. "Don't leave her alone," the nurse was told. Around ten at night, Baby felt that something had come out of her. She asked the *ayah* if the baby had been born. The *ayah* and nurse burst out laughing. Then, suddenly, she got such a huge cramp that she became mad with pain. Had her hands and feet been free, she would have picked up whatever she could find and shattered it to pieces. The *ayah* said, "Poor thing, she is in such pain but nothing is happening." Then she told Baby, "Turn your mind to God, or to Maha Kali, and everything will be all right." Baby did as she was told. "Oh, God, *jai Ma Kali*," she cried out, "your Baby can take no more! Please, either cure her or take her away, but don't leave her to suffer like this." Along with the prayer came another spasm of pain so strong that all Baby could do was to shout, "Ma!"

The *ayah* and the nurse were standing at the foot of the table. The nurse said to the *ayah*, "I can see the head, but the baby is not coming out." And so saying, she ran to fetch the doctor. By this time, Baby had taken leave of her senses. The doctor came and tied Baby's stomach with a belt and then he felt the stomach and said the child had turned. The nurse fetched another doctor. Baby's hands and feet were jerking with the pain, and she was straining so much that her bonds broke. Quickly, four people came and tied her up again. She continued to scream for her mother, "Ma, oh, Ma! I'm dying, Ma! Save me, Ma! Where are you?"

The doctor caught hold of the baby and pulled it out. Suddenly Baby's screams and wails died down and she became still. The passage had ruptured and had to be stitched up, and the nurse brought what seemed like frightening-looking scissors and knives to the doctor. Fearfully, Baby asked the *ayah*, "What is he going to do with all that? I am perfectly all right now."

"It's nothing. Just lie still like a good girl." Baby lay there, listening to the child's whimpers. "Your son has been born on a good day," the *ayah* said. "It's ten minutes after ten on the night of Janamashtami, and his weight is not too bad, either: three kilos and ten grams." And talking away like this, she kept Baby distracted while the doctor did his work. Once he was finished, he told the *ayah* that she could clean up. Oh God, there was so much blood—buckets full of it! Can one still have any strength after losing so much blood? "Clean her up properly," the doctor said, and left.

After the doctor had left, they took Baby off the table and tried to stand her up, but she fainted and fell to the floor. The *ayah* ran to call the doctor. The moment he came back, he said he was afraid something like this would happen. Then they picked Baby up and put her on a stretcher and took her to a bed. All Baby was aware of was faint voices in her ears, but she could not speak or even see anything. They tried to put her on a drip, but they could not find a vein in her hand. Another doctor then came along and said, "Here, let me do it." He turned her hand this way and that and found a place and pushed the needle in. He then told the nurse that when one bottle finished, she should put a second one on. The nurse did that with first one, then another and then a third bottle and then she went away, telling the other patients that even if Baby asked for water, she should not be given it. In the dead of night, when Baby awoke, she felt fine but when she tried to get up she couldn't. Her body felt as if there were nothing in it: she felt light and thin and as if she were glued to the bed. And she was very thirsty. She asked for water, but no one would give her any—they had been told not to. Just then, Baby noticed a bottle on a table nearby. She was beginning to feel that if she did not drink water she would die. She managed to stretch her arm out and grab the bottle, and drank all the water down in one go. In the morning when she woke up, she saw that her eyes and face were terribly swollen. When the doctor saw her he shouted at her: "Do you want to die? Why did you drink that water?" Baby could only weep. She had no answer.

A little while later, the *ayah* brought Baby's child and handed him to her, and then she demanded money to buy sweets. "Your first child has been born on such a good day: a Wednesday, and the birthday of the god Krishna. When will his father come? We have worked so hard, we've been awake all night, and you had such a difficult time as well."

Baby said, "Sister, I am terribly hungry." The *ayah* went away and brought her some tea and bread and gave it to her, saying, "It's time to feed the child." Baby ate the bread and drank the tea, but she was still hungry.

"Yes, and so you will be," the *ayah* said, "after all, everything's gone out of your body." Then she changed the subject and asked again, "Isn't anyone coming from your home?" She had barely said this when Baby's husband arrived. The moment he appeared, the *ayah* said to him: "Look, Baba, we've stayed awake all night for her. Now give us our due."

Baby's husband was delighted at the news that a son had been born to him. The nurse came and saw him and said, "Aha, look at the smile on the face of the father! Is there no one at home who could have spent the night with her here? If she had died yesterday, then who would have been there to eat this food that you have brought? You're lucky that she survived because we had no hope that she would. What kind of man are you that you left her to suffer so much, and for so long, and without even bothering to show your face?" Baby's husband listened to all this without a word. Baby said to him, "Show me what have you brought. I don't know whether I will be able to eat anything or not."

The *ayah* said, "You need to give her support, she is still very weak. Feed her some good things. It's not enough to give your attention to the child. The child's mother also needs to be looked after." A woman lying in a nearby bed, who was still in the hospital after delivering her child, repeated the same thing. Baby's husband had brought some rice and dal from home and some fish curry from a restaurant. The child started to cry. Baby put him to her breast, but she had no milk. "First you should eat your fill and then the milk will begin to flow," the *ayah* told her. "Until then, you should give him water with sugar in it. I'll bring you some warm water." Baby's milk began to flow after two days.

She was feeding the child when the doctor came. Startled, Baby put the child down. The doctor said, "Are you all right? You have had to suffer a lot. And look at your age, too! Why did you choose to have a child so young?" She did not answer. She kept looking around, unable even to say the child was crying and she needed to feed him. The *ayah* picked up the crying baby and gave him to her, saying, "Look at this, the child is crying. What kind of girl are you? You should be feeding him. I see that you know nothing at all! Tell me, how on earth will you bring this child up?" Then, her voice softened, "I think they will let you go home today. Make sure you give us our due before you go. Even if I am not here, you can pay whoever is on duty at the time. Don't run away without paying, okay? Remember, we are the ones who have to clean up after you and there's no way that can be paid back, but at least leave something for us."

The next day the doctor came around eleven o'clock. "And how are you feeling today?" he asked Baby gently. "We're going to release you in the evening. You can leave with someone from your home. I'll write you a prescription for medicines you need to take: just remember to take them at the right time and don't work too much, all right?"

Around noon, Baby's parents came. When they did not find

her in the delivery room, they went outside. She was lying on a corner bed. When she saw them she called out to her stepmother, "Ma, I'm here."

"I've been looking for you everywhere," she said. "Your Baba is waiting outside."

"Who is this?" asked another patient.

"My mother," Baby said.

Surprised, she said, "My God, I find that hard to believe."

"It's a boy, isn't it?" Ma said, "You remember I told you it would be a boy? Go and show him to your father." As Baby got up to go, another patient asked her, "Who has come? Is that your mother?" Then she turned to her mother and said, "So, *Didi*, aren't you happy with your little *nati*, your grandson? Is he good enough for you to marry, do you think?'

And Ma smiled and said, "He certainly is."

As Baby went out with the child, she saw her father, who cried out, "Don't bring him here! Don't!" As she continued to walk toward him, again he said, "Look at this girl! I told you: don't bring him here. I will look at him at home." Shortly after Ma and Baba left, Baby's husband showed up. Baby told him that the hospital had released her. "Then let's go home," he said. "Wait, I will get a rickshaw. In the meanwhile, put your things together." He walked off and then came back and told her to eat the rice that was there in the tiffin box. When Baby's parents had come they had brought with them a cousin of Baby's, Sadhna, the daughter of Baby's aunt. They had asked Sadhna to go with Baby to help with the child, so when the rickshaw came, they all got into it and went back to Baby's home.

THE RICKSHAW STOPPED OUTSIDE THE HOUSE AND AS usual, when I saw what a state the house was in, I didn't want to go in. Sadhna told me to wait outside while she cleaned up, so I sat outside with the child. Sandhya-di came when she saw me. Smiling, she asked me, "How are you? How does your body feel?"

"I'm okay now, but I feel very weak."

"That'll be there for a while. You've gone through a lot. Had it been anyone else, she probably would have given up long ago." Then, raising her voice, she said, "Oye, Shankar, it's not enough to just look at the boy, you'll have to look after his mother as well. Make sure you feed her properly." Then she turned to Sadhna and said, "First light the fire and make a cup of tea for your Didi."

The child was in my lap and suddenly he soiled himself. It got onto my clothes and my hands. As soon as I tried to clean one place, another part would get dirty. When Sadhna saw me she said, "Eh ma, what are you doing? Here, let me do it. You're just shifting it from one place to another!" Shamefaced, I looked at her, and then I turned away, smiling. Sadhna knew exactly what to do. Being the elder daughter, she had had to look after her young siblings. "This is all very well, but how long can Sadhna look after your child?" said Sandhya-di. "Finally, you're the one who is going to have to bring him up, so you'd better learn how to do all this."

Sadhna cleaned up the child and handed him back to me, and in a little while she came back with some tea and bread. While I was eating, she cleaned up one corner of the house and made some space for me to lie down. Sadhna, the child, and I would sleep there at night. One night she told me that in her home no one would be allowed to walk in and out of the room where a new mother was before a certain time had elapsed, but I said to her, What can we do? We only have one room.

One day Ma arrived and said to Sadhna, "Come on, it's time for you to go back." I asked if she could stay on for a while—at least till the child was a month old. I said that either my husband or I would take her back, but Ma was adamant. Sadhna didn't want to go, either, but she had to listen to my mother, in whose house she was staying. She left and now I had to manage everything on my own: the housework, looking after the baby, everything. All the neighbors wondered where Sadhna had gone. Why didn't she stay on a bit longer, they asked; it would have been good if she had. But what could I do? She had come to visit my parents, and if they did not want her to stay with me any longer, I had no say in the matter. Some of them told me to be careful, especially with water, because I was still weak and could catch an infection. They were all so supportive of me, much more so than my Ma and Baba had been, that I sometimes marveled at it. Ma and Baba had come only once since I'd been back from the hospital, and even then it was only to take Sadhna away. And not once did they ask how the child was.

I had to continue to bear all these troubles. My child was barely a month old when my milk began to dry up. The baby would cry from hunger and I could not understand why. A neighbor once asked me, "Why is your child crying so much? Does he not get enough to eat? Why don't you give him some other milk and see?" I mentioned this to the child's father, but for several days, he completely ignored me. Then one day, I don't know what came into his head, but he went out and came back with a tin of milk powder. And with my milk and this milk, the child seemed to be satisfied. We needed to get three tins in a month. Whether we ate or not, the child had to be fed. If I asked my husband for anything else, he'd lose his temper and there would be tension in the house.

TIME PASSED LIKE THIS AND THEN ONE DAY, MY BROTHER and my elder uncle and a friend of theirs named Dharni Kaku arrived at our house. At the time, I was lying down with my child, so I quickly got up and made room for them to sit. "I won't sit, child," Uncle said.

"Whyever not? What's wrong? Why is your face looking so pinched?" I asked. Uncle did not reply, so I turned to Dharni Kaku, but he also remained silent. Finally I asked my brother, "What's wrong? Why don't you tell me what it is?" He told me only that our sister was no more and then he began to weep. "Which sister?" I asked him.

"Our Sushila Didi," he said. But I couldn't understand what could have happened to Didi. As the implications of what he had said sank in, I felt a chill spread through my body. I stood as if rooted to the ground. Dharni Kaku repeated the news two or three times and suddenly I screamed. I ran straight out of the house all the way to Baba's place. There, I beat my head on the ground and wailed, "Baba, now we've lost Didi as well. First it was Ma—and she's there and not there—and now it is Didi. We thought even if we don't have a mother, at least we have an older sister. And now she's also gone." Baba held my arm and lifted me up and told me gently to calm down. "I'm going to find out what has happened," he said.

"But what's the use?" I asked him. "No one ever bothered to find out anything about her." Every time I went to see Didi, her neighbors would ask if her father had completely forgotten her, for he never went to see her. Was it because of his new wife, they asked, that our father now had no time for his own children? I told Baba that he had no idea how sad it made my sister to have to listen to all these things. "And now look at you. You never really cared about her," I said to him between sobs.

When I had run off to see Baba, my uncle and Dharni Kaku left to see my elder brother, who lived in a nearby village with his wife. When Uncle got there, he found my brother just sitting down to eat. He started to rise, but Uncle said to him, "Son, finish your meal first." When my brother's wife saw everyone she started to light the fire again but Dharni Kaku said to her, "Daughter, there's no need to cook for us." My other brother had left Uncle and Dharni Kaku at my brother's house and gone to give the news to Grandma. My brother sat back down to eat and was halfway through his meal when my grandma arrived. "*Arre*, Ajay, what is this I hear about your Didi dying?" My brother was shocked. Dharni Kaku said to my grandma, gently, "Look, we just arrived here, and didn't want to tell him anything at least until he had finished eating. But you've just come and blurted everything out." My brother left his food half eaten and ran to meet Baba.

I was with Baba at the time. When my brother arrived, his eyes were bloodshot and it looked as if he were ready to kill someone. He couldn't even cry. It took quite a while for the tears to come. He was watching Baba strangely: here was a man who had just lost his elder daughter, yet there was not a tear in his eye. Suddenly my brother began to cry loudly. Dharni Kaku tried to comfort him, but it was no use and the more he cried, the more my tears fell. When he had run off to meet Baba, Grandma had followed him. Now, wiping her tears, she said to him, "I have never seen your father lift a finger to help your sister. It was only when we forced him that he took the trouble to find out about her."

"But none of us bothered about her," said my brother, "that's why that bastard thought that there was no one to care for her." Then, softly, he asked Uncle, "What happened to Didi, Uncle?"

"Mangal came to see me," explained Uncle, "and he told me that she was very unwell and we should go to see her."

Mangal was my Didi's husband. This was all he told Uncle and then he disappeared. Uncle's wife asked after the children, but he did not even stay to answer. As he was leaving, Uncle asked him what was wrong with Didi and all he said was that she had smallpox. Uncle did not even stop to eat anything: he just rushed off straightaway to see Didi. But when he got there, he found her lying wrapped in a sheet in the courtyard. He was shocked, and the fruit he had hurriedly picked up for her fell from his hands and scattered on the ground. He had taken along a tender coconut to offer her so she could bathe with its healing water, and that, too, fell from his hands. There was no sign of her husband: it seemed he had disappeared after he went to Uncle's house. My heart was hammering in anger at hearing this story but Baba's eyes were still dry. Once, in anger, Didi had said to Baba, "How can a father be like this? It's as though I have already performed my father's last rites, his *shraadh*." And now Baba kept repeating, "Now we'll see who will do whose *shraadh*."

Grandma chided him: "Is that all you can think of at a time like this? Your daughter has died and you have not the slightest concern or sorrow for her."

"No, Didi, that's not what I mean . . ."

"What are you saying then?" she interrupted him. "Your daughter is dead and instead of going there straightaway you're wasting your breath here wondering who said what to whom . . ."

"Yes," Uncle said angrily, "do you want to go there or not? Otherwise tell me and I will go."

"No, Dada, of course I will go. I do want to. But will my daughter still be there? Won't they have taken her away?"

"No, I have told them and I have left Raju there with her, and have told her to make sure no one takes our girl away before we come." Raju was my elder aunt.

"So I will be able to see my daughter?" Baba asked.

But those people had put enormous pressure on my aunt and had forced her to let them take the body away. First they said they could not keep a body in the house for so long. She tried to insist that they wait for Uncle and Baba, but then they threatened her and forcibly took the body away. Before anyone from our family could get there, they had completed all the rites and cremated the body. She could do nothing. My uncle and Baba took a long time to get there because they had first to take a train and then walk for three miles. When they finally arrived, my aunt ran out crying, saying to Uncle, "Dada, I was not able to keep my promise! I could not do as you asked. They forced me to let her go!"

The moment I heard the news about Didi, I'd left everything and run off to my father's house. When I got home, my husband was sitting on the kitchen stool with the baby. When he saw me he said, angrily, "Have you no sense at all? Leaving such a small baby and running off like that!"

"But I knew you were at home," I said. Just then, Sandhya-di saw that I was back so she came across and said, "What is all this? What happened?"

"My sister is no more and I am in such a sorry state that I can't even offer to look after her children. They'll be so bereft. I know what it is like to be a motherless child. Who can they turn to when they are hungry or in need? We have a mother, yet we have spent our lives being motherless. These children will also suffer like we did."

"Can your father not keep them with him?"

"Do you think those people have any idea how to bring up children? I don't know what they're thinking of. We'll only find out when they come back from Didi's house."

"All right, we'll talk later. Now it's time you fed your own child."

I put the baby to my breast and as he suckled, my thoughts turned to Didi. Had my mother been alive today, how much she would have wept to see her daughter gone. But this new mother of ours had not shed a single tear. What would Didi's children do now? They must be devastated. There was no one to feed them, to comfort them now. If they wept, their father would probably beat them. Or that family would treat them like animals and throw them out of the house. "Get out of here," they would say. "Who do you think you are?" Imagine those children's shock and grief— who would they turn to? The same fate awaited them that we had lived through. I looked at my child and wondered what life held for him.

After a couple of days of this, I announced to my husband that I wanted to go to my father's house.

"But you said they were not there, that they'd gone to Didi's place, so what will you do there?"

"Grandma is there, and I want to go and find out what happened." So off I went, and the very next day Baba and Ma came back. Ma went in straightaway to bathe. The moment Baba saw me he put his bag down on the floor and his eyes filled with tears. I began to weep and in between my loud sobs, I asked him to tell me what had happened to Didi. He held me and said, "Child, don't cry. I've lost my daughter, and I keep thinking how difficult her life must have been."

"Stop crying now," Grandma said to me. "What's happened has happened. Crying will not bring her back, will it?"

"Oh, Didi," Baba said, "she had to bear so much. That bastard Mangal was carrying on with someone else. And if my daughter said anything to him, he would beat her. Some people there were saying she took poison; others said she was ill. So many stories. But I asked her little boy to tell me what had happened. At first, he was a little scared and would not talk to me. I felt so sorry for him, poor little child, he's only five. Then I picked him up and took him out, and spoke to him there. Slowly he told me . . . Grandpa, he said, there was nothing wrong with her. I told him, quickly, tell me what happened, I'll take you with me. Do you want to come? Yes, the child said, you promise you will take me? I said, Yes, yes, and you will stay with Grandmother. Now tell me what happened. I'll tell you, he said, but you must promise not to tell my father. I promised that I wouldn't let anything happen to him. Then, slowly, the child started to tell me his story. This is what he said: 'Do you know Grandpa, that for three or four days now Baba had been fighting with Ma and beating her. Yesterday he locked the door of the room and beat her up very badly. I was in the room at the time. When Ma began to shout for help, Baba caught hold of her throat and began to strangle her. When her tongue started to come out, I cried out: Baba, stop, she will die, let her go, my Ma will die . . . and I began to howl and beat him on his back but even then he didn't stop. When Ma's voice was completely gone and she could not speak anymore, he let her go and she fell with a thud to the ground. Then he began to call out to her but she did not reply.' I asked him, 'What happened next?' "

Perhaps Baba thought that Didi had not died then, that there was still some life in her, so he asked again what happened. The child told him that after that, his father had pushed him out of the room and gone away himself. Then he was crying so hard he could not say any more. Baba asked the neighbors and they told him that Didi hadn't survived the beating.

Baba's eyes now filled with tears. "Oh, Rani," he said to Ma, "my poor child, they strangled her to death. What did she do to deserve this? I'm going to see that bastard goes to jail for this." Later, Baba's neighbors and others told him that when Mangal heard of this threat, he said, "So what? Let him send me to prison. I'll make sure that not one sign of that woman is left in this world." Baba understood this to mean that he would kill off their children when he came out of prison. We discussed this a lot. Baba was angry that they had not waited until he came to cremate her: he would have made sure the body was sent for a postmortem. He felt really helpless. Many of Baba's friends in the neighborhood had offered to help, saying he only had to say the word and they would cut off Mangal's hands so his life would effectively be finished.

Everyone listening to this story had tears in their eyes. Baba could hardly speak, he was so overcome with sorrow and rage. I kept thinking of how she must have felt, the fear in her mind as she watched her husband killing her. Listening to Baba made me want to scream. He was telling us how they had refused to let him take the children away. Finally Baba had left, saying that if God willed, the children would have a good life. But I thought, whether God willed it or not, my sister must have had such a hard life.

After a few days, life returned to normal at Baba's house. He no longer seemed to be concerned about what Didi's children were going through. Sometimes I wondered if he even realized that he had two other grandchildren. I wanted to go and see the children, but how could I? I was helpless and tied to my husband. I had to do as he said, I had no independence. But why? I used to wonder at the injustice of this. It was *my* life, not his. Did I have to behave as he wanted simply because I was with him? He treated me as if I were an animal. If I had no happiness and peace in his house, was it necessary that I should stay on there in that living hell?

A week went by like this in Baba's house. But I was not happy. Ma and Baba did not tolerate me sitting down anywhere even for a short while. Baba did not mind if Ma did what she wanted, but as for us—my brother and I—he always complained. Some days, if I was not feeling well and wanted to rest, Baba seemed quite unconcerned. But if I lay for a little while in bed, he just would not stand for it. I had to do all the housework when I was there, and if I overstayed my welcome even slightly there would be all sorts of tensions in the house, and I would have to go back to my husband. This is exactly what happened this time.

MY CHILD WAS SOME THREE MONTHS OLD WHEN ONE DAY, after we had eaten, I was cleaning outside the house when my husband looked up and said, "Oh, there's Baba." Baba? I wondered, whose Baba? I thought perhaps he meant my father had come, but he pointed and said, "Look, look over there." I looked, and saw an old man dressed in white. He stood there looking at me and my husband. I was surprised. Then my husband ushered him inside and I quickly got some water to wash his feet. He went in and began to talk to his son while I stayed outside. I could hear a bit of what they were saying: "You got married without telling any of us," his father said. "But why? Not only did you not tell anyone, but it's been three years and you have not so much as shown your face at home. And all the time your mother keeps asking after you. We wanted so much to have your marriage at our house, to bring our daughter-in-law home, and yet you did not say a word, and you even had a child without telling us. Don't you think you owe us at least this much?" After a while he continued: "If this is what you feel, then tell us. We won't bother you again and we'll not feel bad about it. We'll just tell ourselves that we have no son." My husband muttered something in reply, but I could not make out what it was. I quickly lit the fire and made tea and took it in to him with a biscuit. My father-in-law seemed very angry with me, but what had I done? I had no idea my husband even *had* parents: he had never so much as spoken of them.

Father and son continued to talk and I listened. I wanted very much to take the child and put him in his grandfather's lap, but I was not sure if I should. How would he take it, I wondered? What if he rejected the child? Shouldn't I at least try? So I just picked the baby up and put him in his lap, saying, "Your son may have been unjust to you, but why punish this innocent child for that? Take him in your arms." My father-in-law smiled gently and his anger vanished. So I left the child with him and went off to cook. I put on the rice and asked my husband what I should make. He told me to wait while he went to fetch some fish.

"Daughter-in-law," my husband's father said to me after he had gone, "when you married my son did no one think to ask whether he had a family or not? Or was it that your father saw a lone man and just married you off to him?"

"Baba," I said, "I know nothing about these things."

"Where is your father?" he asked. "Where is his home?"

"It's quite close by. Perhaps you could go there tomorrow morning with your son?"

"How old is my grandchild now? Have you given him a name?"

"He's three months old and, no, I have not yet found a name for him."

"So, then we will call him Subal. I have six children," he added, "and only my eldest son is married, although he is so unfortunate that he's had no male child: one after the other there have been only girls. My middle son is not yet married and after him is your husband. You don't even know anything about our work. We are potters. What is your father's name?"

"Upendranath Halder."

"Oh, so you are Halders, are you?" I murmured a yes and he continued, "So does he come here to meet his grandchild?"

"Yes, but very seldom."

I was talking to him with my head bowed and my sari pulled low over my forehead. After we had eaten that day, he commented to my husband that I was a good cook, even if the food was a little too spicy for him. I was relieved to hear this, and I realized that he was not angry with me anymore.

The next morning, my brother came by and when he saw my father-in-law he called from outside, "Who is that, Didi?" I told him, and then went inside to announce my brother's arrival. "Where is he?" said my father-in-law. "Call him in, call him in." Then he rushed out and invited him to come in for a while, but my brother said he couldn't stay as he was on his way to the market. When he got home and he told my father that my father-in-law had come to visit, Baba was really surprised. "Rani," he said to Ma, "that means Shankar lied to us when he said he had no parents."

"Leave it be," she said. "What can we do about it now? Anyway, now that we know, let's go and meet his father."

In the evening, they came over. Baba called out from outside, "Baby, I hear your father-in-law is here!" I was cooking and Father-in-law was sitting nearby drinking tea. "He's right here," I said, "why don't you come in?"

"Oho," said my father-in-law, "come in, Brother, come in and sit down. Daughter, make some tea for your parents."

"No, no, we've just had tea," Baba protested.

I knew that there was no point making tea, that Baba would not drink it, so I pretended not to hear. "How is everyone at your home?" Baba asked my father-in-law.

"Fine, thank you, everything is fine. Tell me, how is it that you people got your daughter married but you didn't so much as tell us about it?"

"We had no idea that Shankar's parents were alive. He lied to us and told us that he was all alone. Had we known you were there, why would we not have told you? I wouldn't have married off my daughter like this." Then, after a brief silence, Baba asked, "So, will you take your daughter-in-law with you?"

"No, not yet. First I need to get home and tell everyone what has happened. His mother wanted so much to have a proper wedding, to bring home her daughter-in-law . . . and look at this chap! He just ran off without a word and got married."

"But now that it's happened," my mother said, "won't you please give them your blessings so they can live a peaceful and happy life?"

"We'll leave now," Baba said. "Tomorrow morning I will send my son here. Please come back with him to our home."

The next day my brother came and took Father-in-law with him. Ma cooked for him and he enjoyed her food very much—even more than mine, as he told me when he returned. He also liked my father's home and their way of living. The next day he left us, promising to come back the next month.

I'D BEEN TRYING TO FIND A NAME FOR MY CHILD. HIS grandfather had named him Subal; my husband called him Budhan; but I didn't like either. My brother-in-law suggested Gautam, which I quite liked, but in the end, I called him Subroto, and his nickname was Babu.

After he'd been gone a month, my father-in-law came back to fetch me. As soon as he arrived, he asked my husband whether I could return with him.

"How can she just leave like that? We'll need to get her things ready, to get her some new clothes and all that."

"Yes, but I can't wait too long. The crop is ready for harvesting and I need to get back there. If she comes back with me, she can take care of all the household work and your mother can join us in the fields. I don't expect your wife to help us in the fields, but at home . . ."

"All right, but just wait a couple of days. I also need to collect some money that's due to me. Once it comes in, you can go."

I could understand my father-in-law's impatience. Everyone would be busy there, especially as the crop was ready for harvesting. He's left all this and come to fetch me because they need my help, I thought, so I decided to get ready to leave as soon as possible. I had no idea how they expected me to conduct myself there. But I felt so happy—as though I was being taken out on a pleasure trip. But I was also wondering how I would manage alone—who would there be for me to talk to? What would I do if I wanted to talk about private things, things I wouldn't want to discuss with people I didn't know? And if I was busy with household chores all day, who would take care of my child? On top of that, I had no idea how long I was expected to be there.

On impulse, I ran to my father's home and asked Grandma if she could send someone with me to my in-laws' house. "Who?" she asked me. I asked her to send her middle daughter, known to everyone as Mez-budi. Grandma agreed, so I ran to Mez-Budi and asked her, "Hey, Budi, will you come with me?"

"Where to?"

"My in-laws' home."

"Will Ma let me go?"

"I've already asked her. I'll come to fetch you tomorrow morning, so you'd better be ready! We'll have to do some walking, I hope you can manage that." And with that I ran back home.

My father-in-law had told me that in order to get to their home, we would have to walk for about three miles. I was a little worried at this, but then he told me, "I knew this would be difficult for you, so I have asked your brother-in-law to bring a bullock cart to bring you to the house." Sandhya-di came to see me before I left, and she explained to me in detail how I was expected to behave in my in-laws' home.

In the morning I was ready bright and early! I went to fetch Mez-budi and found that she was halfway to our place already! So we set off together and boarded our bus. When we got down at our stop, we saw a man standing with a bullock cart. Mez-budi said to me, "Quick, cover your head!" I promptly did so and we clambered up into the cart. This was the first time I'd ever been on a bullock cart. Mez-budi was dying of laughter at the rocking motion of the bullock cart and I was also quietly laughing into my *aanchal*. My father-in-law followed us on his bicycle. There were large ruts and ditches in the road, and as the bullock cart went over them, it would jerk and rock from side to side. Mez-budi found this very amusing and I kept trying to hush her giggles. The road went on and on—it seemed like forever. I kept asking my brother-in-law how much further it was as we passed village after village.

Finally, we stopped and my brother-in-law said, "Look, there's my elder aunt." I got down quickly and touched her feet. "Come, come into the house," she said. My mother-in-law brought a *charpai* out. Before sitting down I touched everyone's feet. I noticed that my mother-in-law was cooking on a wood fire and I began to get a bit worried—how would I manage? I was used to cooking with coal. After a while, my husband's elder aunt took me to the pond to bathe. I was so happy to see the water, and I wanted immediately to jump in and start swimming, but I stopped myself. What would they think?

The water was beautiful, clear, and as still as a sheet of glass. Some days it was warm and on other days it was cool, and I made every excuse I could to go to the pond. Once in the water, I would jump around and play like a child. People began to ask me if there was no pond where my father lived and I told them that there was, but it was never as clean and clear as this one. One day my younger brother-in-law, Anil, asked me if I knew how to swim. I said yes, so he said, "Let's go to the pond and see who can cross it faster."

"Okay, let's go!"

The pond was quite wide, and we got into it together and began to race. He gave up halfway across, but I reached the other side in a flash! People on the banks were amazed. Who would have thought that a city girl could swim so well? Others remarked that this was the first time that they'd ever seen anyone swim all the way across. Some even came home and talked to me afterward. Many people in the neighborhood began asking my father-in-law questions about me. "Why," they said, "is this your daughter-in-law or your daughter? She doesn't even cover her head in front of you."

"What of it?" said my father-in-law. "I'm the one who has asked her not to. She is like my daughter." And it was true: he had asked me not to bother covering my head in front of him, only to make sure that it was covered if others were around, because, as he explained, "this is a village and people are not so open-minded." In fact, people there were curious to see if a city girl like me could manage the housework. Both my father-in-law and mother-in-law assured them that I could, and my husband's elder aunt also told them that she thought I was good-natured. Everyone there was kind to me and seemed to like me.

I liked my father-in-law's large house with its open courtyard. Their fields were also large and provided enough rice to feed the family all year round. While I was there, each morning, I would be the first to wake up; I would clean and tidy up, and then make everyone's tea. By this time the others would be awake, and getting themselves ready for the day. They often remarked that before I came into their household, their tea was never ready so early in the morning. They even asked me to stay on there for longer, but I wondered whether I could. I couldn't tell them, of course, but my cousin was not at all happy there and she kept insisting that we go back.

I had more than my share of importance because I had a son, and they gave him a lot of love and affection in that house. There was an elder daughter-in-law in the family also, but there were problems between her and her husband and no one talked to them properly. They lived apart in a room of their own in the house, and also cooked separately. I had decided that I would not get caught up in any family politics and would talk to everyone, so I did. The others did not like this, and they made that quite clear. I listened to what they said but did not let it affect me. Their dispute was mostly over property, and the elder brother-in-law was of the view that since he had now separated from the family, they should hand over his share of land to him. His father, however, felt that while he was still alive, he would remain the sole owner and there would be no division of the property. They fought repeatedly over this.

Meanwhile, my sister-in-law tried to make ends meet by making preparations out of flat rice and selling them. I did not like to see her going through such hardship. One day, while I was still there, father and son fought bitterly and the son lashed out at his father. I was watching this spectacle and I felt sick in my heart. I no longer wanted to stay there. A few days after this incident, I asked my father-in-law if he would take me back—I told him my cousin was insisting upon it. Grandma urged him to let me go, because my husband was alone and needed me. My father-in-law said, "I can't let her go just like this. We need to get her some new clothes—otherwise what will her parents say?" I told him not to bother with such things, and that my parents would not even get to know.

Days passed, and we kept putting off my departure. A month had gone by since my arrival there. They were happy to have me there: I took over all the housework and they were free to work in the fields. One day my cousin asked Anil if he would come with us to climb the hills nearby. "But will you be able to climb up?" he asked.

"Let's go and see," she said. So Anil turned to me and said, "Come along, Boudi, let's go!"

I wasn't sure I'd be able to walk that far, but he insisted. "Of course you'll manage. Come on!" The hill looked as if it was close by but as we set off towards it, it seemed to recede into the distance. Finally we made it there. Looking up, it seemed so huge, I wondered how on earth we would manage to climb up. Apart from anything, I had my child with me. Anil took him from me, perhaps because he thought I would not be able to make it carrying a baby. But my cousin and I more or less ran up the slope and he was left far behind! When we got to the top, he called out, "Boudi, quick, come down!' He sounded frightened, so we rushed down, tripping and falling, but when we got there, we found he was laughing. "Why are you laughing?" I asked him.

"Are you so frightened of *langurs*?" he asked.

"Did you see any?"

"Oh, God, you just saw *langurs* and look at the state you are in!" he laughed. He didn't even give us time to look down from the top and see the little houses dotted around. And of course we weren't scared of *langurs*: there were so many of them in our old home in Dalhousie, they'd often come right up to our door!

When we got home, everyone asked if I'd managed to climb up.

"I thought she wouldn't be able to," said Anil, "but she managed to even leave me far behind!" They were all surprised at how a city girl could outdo their village girls so easily. My mother-in-law said, "She is more like Manhar's [my father-in-law's] daughter than his son's wife."

I hadn't seen such a wide-open and empty place before. Things were so spread out that even if you had to buy salt you needed to walk nearly half a mile to get to the shop. It wasn't as if I had not seen a village before; I had, but not one like this. My Didi's father-in-law's home was also in a village, but it wasn't like this. What surprises me is that I managed to spend a whole month in such a place. At first I'd thought I wouldn't be able to spend such a long time there, but gradually everything began to seem possible, so much so that I found I was even able to cook on a wood fire. The only things I did not manage to do were to work in the fields and to roast *mudi*. Had I done so, my in-laws would have been very happy with me, but this wasn't possible.

FINALLY, THE DAY CAME FOR ME TO LEAVE. INSTEAD OF Father-in-law, Anil came to see me home. When we got there we found that everything had changed. Our home no longer stood where it was: instead, new houses had been built in that area. The road now ran a few feet behind our little house instead of in front of it, and Sandhya-di's and our houses now stood side by side. Our veranda touched hers and there was only a thin partition in between. The courtyard was small but still better than the earlier one.

We could see the home of Shashti and her family clearly from this new house. They were three sisters, the eldest was called Shitla, and the middle one, Tushu. I was closest to Shashti, whose real name was Pratima, although I got along quite well with all of them. Shankar did not like me going to their house at all, but I didn't really care. I couldn't understand what was wrong with my going there: they seemed like perfectly ordinary people to me. All three sisters were married, but none of them lived with their in-laws. Shashti, whose son was a little older than mine, was fair and attractive but had lost one eye. I liked all the sisters very much: they were kind to anyone who came to visit them, no matter how important or otherwise the person might be.

One day I asked Sandhya-di why my husband did not like me going to see Shashti and her sisters. She said, "You won't understand," but I persisted. "Can't you see that although they're all married, not one of them lives with her husband?"

"But does that make them bad?" I asked.

"Listen, I'll tell you their story. When Shashti's elder sister got married, she asked her husband if her mother could stay with them and he agreed. A little later Shashti and her younger sister went to visit them, and they stayed on there. The brother-in-law called his mother-in-law 'Ma,' and treated his sisters-in-law like sisters. He arranged both of their marriages. But the younger one was unable to live in her new home. After her elder brother-in-law died, she found it difficult to shoulder the burden of two families, and she was really disturbed to see a relationship developing between the older brother-in-law's widow and his younger brother. She tried to argue her case, but to no avail: so eventually she came back to her mother's home, where she's been ever since.

"As for Shashti herself, well, when her husband's first wife died he remarried in order to have someone look after their son. But after they'd been married for a while, he left home, saying he was going away on work and would return later. She wrote to him several times while he was away and every now and again he would write back. One day, he came back and stayed with her for nearly a year. Then he took her to her mother's home and left her there saying he would return shortly to take her back to their home. Shashti was pregnant at the time. He never came back."

So this was the story. What I still couldn't understand was

how any of this was the sisters' fault. I knew my husband did not like me going to visit them, so I would visit them when he was not around and he would be none the wiser. I thought, why shouldn't I go there? I didn't think there was anything wrong with them, and they were kind to me and my child. Shashti and her mother were both very religious, and Shashti often became possessed by the goddess. I used to wonder how she could be bad if the goddess could enter her. One afternoon, I was at their house when suddenly my husband came home. Shashti's mother said, "Look, Shankar's come home! Go, go home at once!" I grabbed my child and rushed home, full of fear. He didn't say a word when he saw me, but roughly caught me by my hair and started kicking and beating me. Then he began to shout and curse: "You bitch," he shouted, "I told you not to go there and you won't listen." Curses and blows rained down upon me. People walking past on the road could see what was happening, but no one stopped him. In fact, some of them even seemed to be enjoying the spectacle. I lay on the ground quietly, while my child wept with fear. None of this stopped me from visiting the sisters.

Our neighbors said all sorts of things about these women that I found difficult to understand. They claimed that men went to visit them, but I wondered, what was wrong with that? After all, women visited them, too. I refused to think of them negatively. They were also women like me, and for me, as a woman, to think of other women in this way has never been possible, nor will it ever be.

There was a community leader called Pratap who often went to visit them, but that didn't seem to make any difference to the respect people had for him! It was always the women who were judged differently. I often wanted to ask why this was so, but somehow I could not bring myself to do so. Perhaps they thought the same things about me, too. In fact, most of these people were preoccupied with who was going off with whom, whose daughter had run away with whom, whose wife was seen talking to whom, and so on. Most of them were petty and could not stand to see someone doing well. I felt very bad about this because, as far as I could see, if everyone did what they wanted to, why should anyone else object?

I SUPPOSE THAT, LIVING IN A PLACE LIKE THAT, IT WAS inevitable that I would come across a man like Ajit. He lived across the road from us, and called me Boudi. He was very pleasant and open with all of us, and often played with my son, buying him sweets and little toys at the local shop. But then all this became excessive and I soon figured out what he had on his mind. I tried to tell him that he should keep his distance, otherwise people would talk. But he said he didn't care and he would do what he wanted. The more I tried to stop him talking to me, the more he pursued me. I was really worried that my husband would misunderstand all this and take it out on me. I began to keep a lookout for him, and the moment I knew it was time for him to come home, I'd go across to a neighbor to visit. But he was cleverer than I thought. He'd hang around waiting until he found out where I was and would turn up there unexpectedly. And for no fault of mine, I became the bad woman in the neighborhood, while he got away scot-free.

My husband beat me up time and again and I tried to ask him why it was I who was getting the beating, and why not the man who was harassing me. After all, to begin with he was my husband's friend and used to come to see *him*. Finally, I decided I would not stay silent any more and I began to answer back when my husband threw accusations at me. We spent nights fighting and screaming at each other. I hated the language he used; I hated being beaten; I simply wanted to pick up my things and run away.

There were times when I told him this and went off to Baba's place. But after two or three days, Baba would bring me back and leave me there.

One day Baba saw Ajit hanging around my house and called him over. "What do you want, son? Why do you come here? Don't you realize that because of you, this poor girl has to face so much violence?"

"But her husband used to beat her earlier also. Why are you saying it's because of me?"

"Yes, I know, son. Perhaps it's neither your fault nor hers. Perhaps it's just fate. I had no idea this bastard Shankar would be like this: he seemed so straightforward when we first met him. But please listen to me, son, and keep away from her." And with this he went away.

Some of my neighbors then spoke to Ajit's father and told him in no uncertain terms to keep his son away from me and my child. For a few days this made things better, but soon enough Ajit was up to his old tricks again. I stayed away even from his shadow and the moment I knew he was somewhere around, I would make sure I went in the other direction, but he simply lay in wait for the chance to set eyes on me, and would start harassing me again. If I went somewhere, he would be there on the road waiting for me; if I changed direction, there he would be again. Sometimes I was so angry that I shouted vile abuse at him and did not stop even at abusing his parents. But all this made no difference at all.

One day Shashti and her mother called Ajit to their home and asked him why he was constantly after me like this. "Can't you see," they said, "how much violence she has to face because of you?"

"You cannot imagine," he told them, "how much I love her."

"But she is married and has a child."

"So what?" he said. "I still love her."

The next day Shashti told me all this. I said, "I see. He says he loves me, and this is what love means for him, does it? That he can watch me being beaten, be the cause of it, and still think nothing of it? Is this what love is all about? Does he have any idea at all what love means? I hate him and I spit on him! Please tell him this, Shashti: I don't even want to set eyes on his shadow!"

But instead of backing off, he became even more persistent. Everyone tried talking to him, but he was adamant. Some people even took it upon themselves to beat him up, but the result of this outburst was that the whole thing became a public issue and even those who knew nothing about it were now in the know. They began to debate who was more at fault, Ajit or I. Some would say it's the girl, others would say it's the boy. The whole thing became a real *tamasha*.

While all this was going on outside, I locked myself within the four walls of my home and wept. I began to think that perhaps there was something wrong with me after all: maybe the whole thing *was* my fault. I knew everyone would be gossiping, and I now hesitated even to leave the house because I didn't know how I would face them all. But, of course, I had no choice. I had to get out of the house: there were all sorts of things to be done. All the time I told myself that if life was going to be like this, it would be better for me to go away. I'd think these thoughts and another day would pass by. My son was three years old by now and I was four months pregnant with my next child. It was hard enough to bring up one child amidst all this, let alone deal with the prospect of another on the way!

ONE DAY THE LOCAL BOYS COLLECTED A FEW RUPEES FROM each household and went and brought a video to watch. When I saw that everyone was contributing, I also gave them a little money. I used to love watching films and *jatras* and so that day, in anticipation, I finished all my housework early. When my husband came home, I asked him if I should put his food out, but he said he wasn't hungry. He kept refusing to eat and time was ticking on. I then asked him again to eat, and I told him I wanted to go and watch a film. He said, there's no need to do so. So I asked him why. After all, everyone in the neighborhood was going and I could go and come back early if he wished. I couldn't see anything wrong with this, but he still refused. I was so angry, I blurted out all kinds of things to him. Then I fell silent: I did not go to watch the video.

In the morning the local girls were full of stories about how good the film was, and one of them turned around and asked me why I had not come. I felt both angry and sad at this. I asked myself what I had done to deserve this, why was there no happiness at all in my life. I thought, *There are families in which the husband and wife get along with each other; they are happy.* People like this must have such a wonderful life. Would my life just stretch out in one long never-ending reel of misery? But it was as if God was deaf to my thoughts.

Then, one day, Shashti's mother called me to their house. When I arrived there, I realized that my husband had followed me. He did not wait to ask anyone anything. Silently, he picked up a stone from the ground and hit me on the head with it. My forehead split apart, and blood gushed out. I just stood there without moving. Shashti's mother began to shout and curse him: "Can you see a man standing here talking to her that you need to hit her like this?" she yelled. "We're all women here, and she's just a slip of a girl. She's barely arrived here and you show up to split her head open?" Then she turned to me and said, "I don't know how you can bear to live with this man. Anyone else would have walked out on him long back."

Quietly, I took my child in my arms and came home. All I asked my husband was what I had done to be beaten like this. The words were barely out of my mouth when he picked up a sturdy piece of wood and began hitting me on my back. A short while later, I felt a piercing pain in my stomach. By the evening it was unbearable and I lay whimpering and crying for my father and mother. The pain was so severe that I could not sit or stand or do anything. I howled in agony all through the night while my husband slept on without a care in the world. Either he did not hear my cries or he couldn't be bothered to do anything about them. I was now shouting, saying I was going to die, but he was utterly indifferent. I begged him to call someone. I told him I had not felt like this even when I gave birth to my child, but he just said, "Who can I call at this time of night?," turned over, and went back to sleep.

In the end, I took my child with me and, clutching my stomach and crying in pain, made it across to the house opposite, where I asked the owner, Mahadev, if he could go and inform my brother of my condition. I pleaded and pleaded with him, saying I was in so much pain that I could not bear it, that if he did not go I would die. "But I don't even know where your Dada's home is," he said.

"Take my son with you: he knows the way."

So, poor man, he held my son's hand and went in search of my brother. Once he got there, he told him I was in a lot of pain and asked him to hurry back.

"But what is Shankar doing?" my brother asked him.

"What do you think?" he replied. "He's fast asleep."

My brother came and put me in a cart and took me away. It was two o'clock in the morning. At that hour, not a single medicine shop was open. We could not find a doctor in the whole of Durgapur. So my brother took me to his house and made me lie down. My sister-in-law began to massage my stomach with oil, but it had no effect. I was in such pain that I wanted to lash out at her and everyone else around. I did not know what to do. My poor sister-in-law went from house to house at that hour of the night and somehow she managed to locate some medicine that could have helped, but even that was of no use. Then my brother brought home a friend of his named Sachin. He pressed my stomach here and there, and then went outside with my brother. After a short while my brother called my sister-in-law out as well. When she came back in she asked when I had last had my period, and I told her it had been four months. Then she asked if I had fallen and hurt myself anywhere. When I said no, she wanted to know how I had hurt myself. I told her that her brother-in-law had beaten me the previous day and since then I had been in this excruciating pain. She said: "You have a child in your womb, but it will not survive. Sachin-da will give you some medicine: it will take around five minutes to work."

But instead of five, fifteen minutes passed and the medicine wasn't working at all. Then Sachin began to worry. He told my brother to rush me to hospital. "We can't save her," he said, "and if you do not get her to hospital, she will die." My brother also started to panic, and quickly got things ready to take me to hospital. Sister-in-law helped me to sit up. Suddenly I felt as if something inside me was slipping out of my body. I became dizzy with fear. My brother's eyes were also wide with fear, and I found I could not make a sound. No matter how hard I tried, no words came out: I could only moan in pain. I could see my brother and sister-in-law standing by my bedside and I could hear Sachin-da saying to them, "What had to happen has happened. Now let's just put her on a separate bed." He turned to my sister-in-law and asked her to give me some hot tea. He asked how I was feeling. I didn't want to talk, but I tried. With difficulty I pushed open my eyes and tried to say something, but I couldn't utter a word. Then they lifted me onto another bed. My brother and Sachin then took away the dirty thing that had come out of my body to throw into the jungle. In the morning sister-in-law woke up really early to go to the pond and wash the dirty and bloodied sheets, and I made my painful way along with her. I had no strength at all in my body, but I knew this was something I had to do. So I waited for her to draw water out of the well and then, with difficulty, I washed the sheets.

The whole day passed in a haze. My husband did not show up at all. Around five in the evening he sent our son over to ask after me. When my boy saw me he said, "Ma, please come home." How ironic that my husband could not find his way to me but my little boy had crossed one neighborhood and found his way into another to see his mother. Even the neighbors commented on this when they heard. They also criticized him for sending the boy so late—It's all very well sending the boy now, they said, but what if she had died in the night? My sister-in-law told me that my father-in-law had come and suggested that I go back home to see him. When I got there I found that my father-in-law had come to take me back to attend a wedding in the family.

I decided to go. My in-laws' home was a place of peace for me. So we left, traveling the same way as last time. At my in-laws' there was a constant stream of people who came to see me: it was as if I were a young bride. We would be constantly talking. It seemed that they liked the way I spoke, even though our dialects were quite distinct, and many words were pronounced differently. I liked the way they spoke and the way they behaved very much.

All the young boys in my in-laws' home were married by now and I found that wherever we went, I was the sister-in-law who was given the most respect. My father-in-law knew, for example, that I did not like to eat *chappatis* at night, so he had told everyone that I should be given rice instead. Sometimes he even said that I should be given rice three times a day if I liked! Despite the kindness and the care I received in that home, every time I went there, something or the other would happen after two or three months that would force me back to my tension-filled home. And every time I left, I felt as if I were leaving my own home—as though I were their daughter rather than a daughter-in-law. I wasn't the only one who was sad: everyone cried to see me go, and I always felt as if I were going somewhere far away from the people who cared for me. But today or tomorrow, I knew that I could not stay at their home indefinitely. My father-in-law was not rich, and everyone had to work in the fields for their living. How then could I be the only one who stayed at home? I couldn't even help in the fields, for I knew nothing of farming and the tasks it entailed.

I had only been back a short while when one day Ma and Baba came from Durgapur to fetch me. But I could not just leave everything and go, so I told them I would come on my own later—their home was not far: it could be reached on foot, or for just three rupees by bus. They made me promise I would come, and Baba told me that he had bought a whole lot of new clothes for Durga Puja—as he did every year—for us. Baba took my sister-in-law with them and on their way back, she told them about how my husband had beaten me up so badly that I had nearly died. When I went to see them they told me, "From now on, you can stay here. There is no need to go back." That was all very well, but how long could I stay? Any visitor who came would soon tire of the tension in that house, and never managed to stay for more than six or seven days. But this time I did not want to leave them, and I told Baba that I would not go back.

A month later, I was still there and my husband had made no attempt to find out anything about me. I had nowhere to go—I did not want to go back to him and it was becoming increasingly difficult for me to stay on at Baba's. In desperation, I told Baba that I wanted to go to my aunt's house. He agreed immediately, and two days later, once he had gotten his salary, he bought train tickets for me and my child and saw us off. We had to travel from Durgapur to Jalangi. Baba had given me 100 rupees and I had even less than that with me.

I went first to my older aunt's house. She was no longer the same person I had known. Her hair was now all matted and untidy. Her five sons were all married and lived separately in the huge house they had. She lived with the youngest son, but would eat with anyone—indeed, whoever cooked first became her host for the day. They were all very fond of me and the moment I got there, they asked why I was on my own. "Isn't Brother-in-law with you? How did he let you come alone?"

"Is there anything wrong with coming alone?" I asked. "Besides, I was at Baba's home and Shankar does not even know I am here."

"But won't he be angry when he finds out?" asked one of my sisters-in-law.

"No doubt. But what will he do? What can he do? He'll shout and scream, and tell everyone that if he gets the chance he'll beat me up. But what else can he do? I don't want to live with him anymore."

"Do you mean that your father married you off without checking on anything?"

"Yes, that's exactly what he did. He always said that he would marry me off to whoever came along, and that is exactly what he did. He did not check on anything. One fine day, Ma's brother came and said to him, 'I have a boy, do you want to give your girl?' and Baba immediately said 'yes.' "

"So what will you do now?" asked my elder cousin.

"I will not go back to him. I would much rather be alone. I have one child. I'll keep him with me and find work somewhere."

There was a woman listening to all this. She was well off, from a neighboring house. She said, "So what will you do now? This is all fate. What was written has happened—your marriage, the child at such a young age . . ." But Aunt interrupted, saying that if it was all down to fate, then why did God give us hands, ears, and all our other faculties?

I had been at my aunt's house for fifteen or twenty days and the time had passed pleasantly. The family there looked after my child and I, and I had even managed to see a couple of films with my sisters-in-law.

I then went to see my younger aunt for a week and then I wanted to go and see my younger uncle in Karimpur. Aunt saw me onto a bus. My uncle was relatively better off than the others: he owned a restaurant and a sweet shop, and his elder son had a shop for tape recorders and radios. They had a large and comfortable house and they ate well. But I sometimes wondered what was the use of that if they had no real love in their hearts for me . . . Still, I went there, and I'd only been there a few days when Baba came to fetch me. I heard him talking to my uncle about me. My uncle was asking my father why he had been in such a hurry to marry me off. "After all," he said, "she's still a child. Why did you have to rush into this? And why did you not tell us? Marriage isn't a game, you know. Traditionally we consider at least five families before we decide, and we take the advice of five elders . . . and you? You didn't so much as ask anyone. You did not invite anyone, we had no information, no news, nothing! You just married her off. You just did as you liked, and now who's having to face the consequences? Not you, but this poor girl! Anyway, there's no help for it now: you'll have to just send the girl right back to her home."

Baba had no answer. The very next day, early, I had to leave with him. Together we went to the *panchayat* house where the elders meet to arbitrate disputes and make other decisions, and Baba sent word to my husband to come there. Five elders were called in as well and in front of them, Baba said to my husband, "See to it now that my daughter is not forced to leave her home again. You must promise to make sure she has everything she needs, and that she never has to leave again." Saying this, he left. I was devastated. On the way back from Karimpur, I had done my best to explain to Baba why I did not want to go back. He'd tried to reason with me, using all kinds of arguments as to why I should go back. In the end, I just gave in. I'd thought, If everyone is saying I should go back, perhaps they are right. Even so . . .

And so I went home with my husband. I found, to my surprise, that we were in a different house altogether. He'd sold the old one to Sandhya-di and taken a new house somewhere deep inside the neighborhood. What I feared had come to pass. I had no wish to live in that overcrowded area: in fact, I would have much preferred to have moved somewhere else altogether. Here, some people spoke to me and others refused to, but either way, it didn't matter to me. I thought, *Well, I'll speak to those who speak to me and not to those who don't.*

AND SO TIME PASSED AND I FOUND MYSELF PREGNANT again. On top of this I was worried about how to send my son to school. How would we manage, I wondered. Eventually we did get him into a school, but it wasn't easy. My husband was no help. He'd gotten into the habit of giving the boy money when he was still very small. Every now and again, he'd hand him fifty paise and the child would take the money and run to the shop. He often missed school because of this, and this led to a lot of tension between us. The child became quite a bone of contention between us, and only I know how much I had to suffer on his behalf . . .

Once, when the child was only three and still feeding at my breast, my husband and I had a fight one day and he beat me up and threw me out of the house, telling me never to return. As I was leaving, he snatched the child from my arms and later, he sent him away to his younger brother's home. I was at my father's home but I couldn't settle down to anything. I missed my child so much and worried about him all the time. Baba brought my little niece and put her in my lap, saying she was also a child and perhaps her presence would console me. But it was no use. Finally, I went in search of my son and when I got to my brother-in-law's home I found him there, playing happily with the other children! I called out "Babu" softly and he looked up and saw me. In an instant, he shot into my arms like a little bird and began grabbing at my breasts with his little hands, trying to pull them toward his mouth. I carried him with me to a temple across the road from their house and let him suckle. As we sat there, a girl of some fifteen or sixteen years of age stopped to watch us. She asked if I was the boy's mother but I did not respond. I thought, *If I say anything, it will lead to more questions*—so I just kept quiet. Soon more girls collected, my brother-in-law's wife among them. "Didi, don't take the child away from here," she said. "His father left us with strict instructions that he is not to go anywhere and also that if you came we were not to give the child to you."

"Why," I said angrily, "does the child belong only to him? Look at him! He's just a baby! He's still suckling. How can you keep him? Do you have any idea of what I have been through without him? And what will you gain by keeping him away from his mother?" She wasn't willing to listen to reason at all, and in the end, she had to snatch the child away from me. He didn't want to leave me any more than I wanted to leave him. I just stood there. After a while, my son came out of the house again, and one of the girls with me said to my brother-in-law's wife, "Why don't you give the child to her? She is his mother, after all. How can she live without her child?"

My boy saw me and started walking toward me. I picked him up and started walking away. Soon I saw that his uncle was coming after us. I walked faster, praying that a bus would come along and we could jump on to it—but there was no bus in sight, and he soon caught up with us. My child howled and cried as my brother-in-law snatched him away from me. I felt like my heart would burst with anger and pain. I did not know what to do. My eyes were streaming with tears as I walked home, forlorn. When I got there, all Baba said was, "So they didn't give you the child, then?" Ma turned to him and said, "She will not be able to survive without her boy." And they were right. I couldn't live without him and I was forced to return to my husband.

By this time I was nearly full term, and I was eaten up with worry: what would I do with a second child when we already had so much difficulty with just one? It was nearly three days since my labor pains had begun and there was no one to take me to the hospital. When Baba learned of this he and Ma came to see me and Baba shouted at my husband, asking if he was bent upon killing me. They had a big fight. My husband hitched up his *lungi* and lunged at Baba as if to beat him. "Stay out of our private lives!" he shouted. Baba and Ma did not utter a word. They just turned and left. A couple of days later, Baba came back. By that time the pain had become much worse and I was in sheer agony. One of our neighbors was with me at that point. She told Baba that he should take me away with him, saying, "Your daughter has suffered terribly these last few days." So Baba got a rickshaw and took me to his company hospital. As he was leaving the hospital, I plaintively asked him, "Baba, will I come out of here alive?" I was thinking of Shashti's brother-in-law, who had gone into the hospital for some reason and had died there. Baba saw the tears on my cheeks and said, "Don't cry, child, everything will be all right. After all, there is a God, is there not?" But when I saw all those sharp instruments in the delivery room, I was terrified. I pleaded with the doctors, "Please don't cut me up!" But they all just laughed at me. Then, like the last time, they tied my hands and limbs to the bed, and took me in. I shouted and screamed, and fainted from fear.

At ten o'clock that night, my second child was born. I woke only around midnight to find myself in a different room, with the child asleep on a small cot beside me. I had no idea whether the baby was a girl or a boy. Gradually, I moved myself from the bed and looked and found I had another boy. I did not know what to do. God gave me another boy, but I had so wanted a daughter! In the morning, I learned from people in the neighboring beds that the child was quite big—some said it was almost as if he was already six months old! The doctor came in and told me that Baba had asked him to operate on me to close up my tubes, but that he had been unable to do so because I was so weak. He also told me that the child weighed 3.1 kilograms.

Ma and Baba came the next day, and Baba was thrilled that he had another grandson! He picked the child up and talked to him, making all kinds of baby noises and calling him "*sala, sala*" all the time. I was eating when the doctor called Baba aside and told him that we would have to wait a month for me to regain my strength before he could operate on me.

I went back to Baba's house. After five days there I felt much stronger. The fifth day was a festival day, Vishwakarma Puja, but I did not stay back. I bathed and dressed, took my child, and went home. I was very concerned about my elder son—I did not want his studies to be disrupted. It had been difficult enough to get him into school and I did not want to fritter away that good fortune. I wanted very much that he, and later my other children, should study and have a proper education.

At home, various neighbors came to see the new baby. One of them looked at the child and said, "My God, look at the size of him! He looks as if he's already six months old!" I was really upset. I thought, *These people say all kinds of things about me, now they're going to start saying them about my child.* So, to ward off the evil eye, I took the little finger of my baby's left hand, sunk my teeth into it, and then spat on his body, saying "*Thoo, thoo.*" Despite this, things kept happening to him all the time. Often I would call in a neighbor named Sitaram. He was like a brother to me, and he knew a lot about spirit possession and different kinds of witchcraft. He'd do all his tricks, dusting the baby, trying to remove evil spirits, and I would then think everything would be all right, but it never was. The child remained sick, and sometimes he got worse. If I told his father, he paid no attention. In the end, it was always I who had to find medicines, pay for them, manage everything. What choice did I have? My parents had tied me to this man. Perhaps the only good thing I can say about him is that he never stinted in his love for the children, and never so much as raised a hand to them. All his violence and aggression were reserved for me.

With two children to feed, our financial situation became tight. I began to think that if I could do something and earn a little bit, that would make things easier and would ensure that there was money to educate my boy. So I thought about it and then asked the neighbors—I thought that if I asked people to send their children to me in the house, I would teach them a bit, and my boy could study alongside as well. That way, I would earn a bit, and also save money on his extra tuition. Little by little people began to send their children to me. Someone paid ten rupees for the month, someone paid twenty, and in this way, I managed to piece together some two or three hundred rupees at the end of the month. Predictably, when my husband saw that I had some money in my hands, he reduced the amount he gave me for household expenses. Nevertheless, I enjoyed teaching, and the children were fond of me. Some of them called me Boudi, the others called me Kaki-ma or Didi, and I decided that even if I earned nothing from them, I would not give up teaching them.

YEARS PASSED. MY ELDER SON WAS NOW IN THE FOURTH or fifth grade. My cousins sometimes came to visit me. One day they brought a man with them who had never been to our house before. "Look, we've brought Dulal with us," they said.

"Who?" I asked.

"Why, don't you remember Dulal? He used to be your neighbor when you lived in that house you rented from the Manis. You used to play so much together."

"Oh yes! I remember! The same boy who had no buttons, or belts, or zips or anything in his trousers? He always held his trousers up with just a thread! And the Manis used to call him Jaamai, Jaamai! That one?" Suddenly it all came back to me! How much fun we used to have, how we used to play together! No sooner had Baba left for work than I'd be out like a shot to play with him. Occasionally, we'd worry that Baba would come back and find us playing and would yell at us. He didn't like me playing at all and if he saw me playing with a boy, that was the end! And that silly Dulal, he only liked to play with girls!

Dulal lived close by, with his brother and mother. At first he used to drop by with my cousins, but then gradually he began to come on his own. I was happy to see him, and often made him a cup of tea or something to eat. He loved the children and they loved him, and the day he did not come, they'd kick up a ruckus pestering me and wanting to know where he was. I knew how they felt. I'd felt the same, I remembered, years ago when we used to play together and sometimes, while playing hide-and-seek, I'd be waiting to be found by him and he'd forget me altogether and go off home to his mother. Now, sometimes when he missed a day, I recognized the same feeling in myself. But of course my husband did not like his coming to our house. Not that he ever said anything, but it was very clear how he felt. Every little action of his spoke volumes. Dalal knew this, too, and one day he told me that he thought one of the reasons my husband treated me so badly was because he did not like him coming to our home. I tried to explain that that was not the case. But I don't think he understood and some days later, he once again said the same thing to me. "Look," he said, "I don't want to become a cause of trouble between the two of you." This time, I lost my temper and turned on him: "That's enough! I don't care about all these things now. Nothing's going to happen because of your coming here. And even if it does, so what? I don't care. Can't I spend time with my childhood friend? What will he do? You think he'll beat me? So what? He's done that plenty of times already. I don't care anymore!"

I guess this must have had some effect, for he continued to come to our home. I knew that he was finding it hard to make ends meet, so I would make sure I gave him something to eat when he came. An uneducated woman, a mother of two . . . I sometimes wondered why I was so concerned for this poor man that I was even willing to risk my husband's wrath. Could an uneducated woman understand this? All she knew was that when Dulal affectionately addressed her as "*tu*," Baby's playful, youthful days would come back to her, and her heart would fill with joy. All she knew was that what she felt was something akin to the feeling her friend Bela had had in her heart for the boy named Tarak, to whom she sent love letters that she'd get others to write. Had she been forced to swear on her children's heads and made to tell the truth, perhaps she, too, would have said that had Dulal known how to read and write, she might have written him similar letters as well.

Whenever Bela heard from her lover, she'd run to me with his letters and I had to read them out to her. I had also read out the first love letter that Tapasi's mother, who lived in the same neighborhood, had been given by a brother-in-law. She had run to me with it demanding, "Tell me, tell me what's written in here." I often watched their faces light up as I read to them, and they'd look at that piece of paper as if their whole life were written upon it. Sometimes I had to write letters for them, too. No matter how much I protested that I hardly knew how to write, I had to write those letters and in the end, I would just do whatever I could.

I also became a sort of confidante and go-between in another relationship between two people in the neighborhood, Vibhuda and Nisha. Vibhuda was married, but he was in love with Nisha. To begin with, his wife and Nisha were friends, but once she realized what was going on, his wife began to hate Nisha, glowering at her all the time and heaping curses on her. I liked them both. Vibhuda's wife was really pretty—one of her feet was smaller than the other but other than that, she was lovely. She often stepped out of the house with her veil pulled low over her face, and everyone thought she was a young bride. She wore a large sindoor mark on her forehead that made her look very attractive. Fair and with lustrous, black hair, she loved Vibhuda a great deal and when he was home, she tried to win his heart by cooking all kinds of things for him. By contrast, Nisha was dark, but she was also beautiful and black-haired. Whenever Vibhuda went out into the neighborhood his wife used to try and follow him, and would ask everyone if they'd seen him talking to Nisha. She often asked me to watch out for them as well. What she did not know was that they often met in my house. Sometimes I worried that she would find out. Often they'd meet there and then go to the cinema together.

One day, a group of us were at a neighbor's house watching television. Vibhuda's wife suddenly arrived and found that both her husband and Nisha were there as well. She did not notice that there were so many others around, she saw only the two of them. She asked Vibhuda to come home but he ignored her. She was furious. It was around eleven or twelve in the morning, and she had just put the rice on to cook at home. She rushed home, and no one knows what she did, but she swallowed something and fell down unconscious. When Vibhuda got home, he found her lying there. A short while later he noticed her trying to take the rice off the fire, but her hands were trembling and she could not get a grip on the vessel. He realized something was wrong and quickly called out to others at home. Between them they rushed her to hospital, but it was no use: she died that night. At first everyone in the neighborhood was surprised, but then the gossip and whispers began. Someone said, She was all right till that morning; someone else insinuated that she had died because of Nisha . . . She was a good woman. Whatever the reason for her death, however, it did nothing to change Vibhuda's feelings for Nisha, and he continued to assiduously woo her and the two of them met frequently. Some months later Vibhuda's elder brother came and arranged a second marriage for Vibhuda.

I learned that Vibhuda was keen to marry Nisha but she was not willing to marry him. I asked her why, and she told me that she could not marry him because the two of them belonged to different castes and if she did, her father would be ostracized from the caste. Whatever the reason, even when he remarried—and he seemed to have married well—he continued to see Nisha and spend time with her. What did happen, though, was that his dead wife now began to plague his new wife. Her spirit would enter the new wife's body and cause her endless grief. Often they had to call an *ojha*, a witch doctor, to rid her of the spirit of Vibhuda's former wife. The *ojha* would sprinkle water on Vibhuda's new wife, then take a flaming torch and try to use its heat to bring the spirit out. Then he'd ask, "Who are you and why are you here?"

"I am his dead wife."

"Why have you entered her body?"

"I will not let my husband get close to anyone. I will not let the child in her womb be born."

Then the witch doctor would frighten her again and she'd agree to leave.

"You promise not to return?"

"Yes."

"And where will you leave from?"

"I'll go out the back way."

Then Vibhuda's wife would run out the back, and collapse in a heap on the ground. This happened to her many times, even though she soon gave birth to a baby daughter. This little girl was the apple of everyone's eye in the family, and she was Vibhuda's particular favorite.

Whatever happened in that neighborhood, one thing was certain: everyone had at least three or four children. If this was the local custom, I seemed to be following it. I would soon be a mother of three. I had decided I did not want any more children after this, and so I was keen to have a daughter. I was determined to have myself operated upon and had told myself that I would not come back from the hospital without having this done. Only Shashti and Dulal knew about my decision. Even Baba did not know, because even though he was aware of my condition, he had made no effort to come and see me. I did not want our family to

grow any bigger. My husband barely gave me any money for running the house and my earnings from the tuitions were also very
variable—some months people would pay, others they would not.

Whatever the case, the most urgent thing at that time was to
organize things for getting to the hospital. This time I was more
prepared. Because I wanted to have the operation I wanted to get
there a bit early, so I'd packed my clothes and kept them ready in
a bundle. I'd asked Dulal if he would keep coming and would
look after my children. Two days before I was to go to hospital,
the pain began. At first it did not seem so bad, so I kept it to myself, but when things began to get worse, I asked my elder son to
go and call Sitaram-da while Dulal stayed with me. I asked my
husband if he would fetch my mother-in-law so that there would
be someone to look after the children, and he did so. Then the
three of them, Sitaram-da, Dulal, and my husband, took me to
the hospital. In a short while I was moved from one room into another. This led to some confusion, for the next morning, when
Dulal phoned to ask after me, he was told that I was not there. He
told everyone in the neighborhood that I had disappeared, and
everyone thought I had run away! As a result, no one came to see
me at all for two whole days.

On the afternoon of the third day—Vishwakarma Puja—I
gave birth to a baby daughter. The next day Dulal again tried to
find out about me and this time he found me with my baby in my
arms. I said, "What happened? Why didn't anyone come to see
me? You all just left me here!" He told me he'd come but had not
been able to find me, and then I told him how, when no one
came, the doctors had assumed there was no one else in my family. Anyway, then he left, and told everyone in the neighborhood
the news: I had had a baby girl.

A couple of days later, I asked the doctor if he would operate
on me and close up my tubes. He said he would prefer to wait till

someone, more specifically my husband, came from my home, so that he could get his permission and his signature on the form. I told him there was no need to wait, that I could sign the form myself. So he agreed and told me to be ready with an empty stomach the next morning. My only worry was who would look after the baby for the three or four days that I needed to recuperate, but fortunately, I had managed to hide away some money, so I was able to get an *ayah* for the child for those few days.

There were seven of us waiting for the operation. I was the first to regain consciousness and the first to recover. Even so, it was fifteen days before I was able to leave the hospital. During this time my husband brought food for me every day, and Dulal also came to see me. When I finally got home, everyone came to see me and they had all sorts of questions. "Where did you disappear to?" they asked. "We heard you were not to be found in the hospital . . ." I had to explain everything to them all over again. I told them I'd been moved to a different room, which is why they hadn't found me when they'd gone there. Several of them also said I was fortunate to have had a daughter after two sons and I thought, *Only I know how fortunate I am!* Whatever my fate, though, everyone loved my daughter. Dulal was especially fond of her and would rush her to the doctor for even the slightest scratch! I was happy, for I could now leave the care of the girl to Dulal and do whatever running around was needed to get my younger son admitted to school. And predictably, soon things came to such a pass that my daughter would refuse to leave Dulal's house and come home.

I had hoped that once I came home from hospital I would be able to get a little rest. But on the contrary, the work only increased. I was also beginning to get this yearning to go away somewhere for a while. Fortunately, my chance came when my younger brother-in-law arrived from Dhanbad and asked me to return with him. "There's a big *mela* on there—why don't you come and visit?" I did not stop to think. I quickly packed a few things, took my children, and headed off to Dhanbad, where I spent a week. We went to the *mela* every day. We wandered around and generally had a good time.

I came back a few days later, happy and relaxed, but shortly afterward our little neighborhood was rocked by a terrible tragedy. A man named Panna had set fire to his wife and burned her to death. She was a beautiful doll-like woman, with dusky skin, curly hair . . . and he just burned her to death! It was a Sunday and she was at a neighbor's house watching television. Panna was drunk—he was often drunk and violent toward his wife. When he found his wife watching television, he was enraged and he caught hold of her and dragged her home. There they must have fought, for suddenly he poured acid on her and searched around for a light to set her on fire. Defiant, his wife picked up a matchbox herself and slapped it into his hand, saying, "If it makes you feel better to kill me, here, go ahead and do it!" Panna was drunk. He took the matchbox, lit a match, and threw it on her. She burst into flames, her clothes burning off her skin, her skin becoming pale . . . she was naked . . . she was still alive when Lata, a neighbor, saw her slumped against the wall in their house and heard her whimpering in pain. She shouted out, calling for help, and lots of people came rushing to their house. We also went there. I saw that she was half-standing against the wall and her skin was blistered with burns . . . she was unlucky enough to still be alive . . .

Panna tried to run away, but the neighbors caught hold of him and locked him up inside the house. The police were called and some people quickly took Panna's wife to the hospital. The police came a couple of hours later and made some inquiries and took Panna away. His wife never came home again. But when questioned in the hospital by the doctors and the police, she refused to blame Panna and said he was in no way responsible for her condition. Till her dying breath, she blamed herself for what had happened!

When they brought her home for the last rites, I went there to see her. Her face was still pale, her bindi in place as always. But her eyes were open, as if she was watching us, and I kept thinking she would speak any moment! I remembered how alive she always looked, how she used to take her two children, a boy of ten and a girl of seven, to school every morning, holding each by the hand. Sometimes if I was outside our house, she would stop by to chat. I wondered what the children would do now, who would look after them. Panna was let out after only three months, but whether he was back at home or not made no difference to anyone. Finally Panna's father-in-law came and took the children away.

Panna went back to work in the gas factory where he had been earlier. He was erratic: some days he went to work, others he just skipped. The house they had lived in was sold, and Panna frittered away whatever he earned on drink. One day we were talking about his wife when Shashti told me that she often dreamed of her, and was frightened because she felt that Panna's wife was standing behind her, looking at her with those eyes that refused to close even in death . . . I got up to leave when Shashti reminded me that there was a puja in her home the next day and I had promised to come. I told her I would be there—I thought that I would pray for Panna's little children at the puja. Shashti's house had an idol of Ma Mansa there and it was to her that I planned to pray, but I determined that I would also keep a fast that day for the goddess. So I did not eat anything all day, and in the evening, as many people collected to fetch water from the pond for the puja, I also got ready to go, but my husband dragged me back home, raining curses upon me. When I asked him why he was behaving like this, he began to beat me. I had fasted the whole day, and I'd bought fruit from the market as an offering, but I wasn't able to do this and that made me really sad. So the next morning I plucked a few flowers and went to Shashti's house to offer them. There were many other girls from the neighborhood there as well. I stood among them, and joined my hands to pray. Suddenly I felt a tug at my hair. I ignored it and continued to pray. But then suddenly someone caught hold of my hair and pulled it so hard that I fell to the ground . . . I turned and saw that it was my husband. He shouted at me, "Come on, you bitch! Get yourself back home!" Like everyone else, I knew that if I went back with him now, he would beat me up thoroughly. So I just continued to pray, and after everything was over, I went home. But even then, I did not go inside, I just stood at the door.

A few minutes later I saw Shashti and a few others rushing to my home, shouting loudly. They were angry. She screamed at my husband: "You can do what you like with your wife, I know it's no business of mine, but you can't come to my house and disrupt things. You disturbed our puja and in front of everyone. How dare you? You've not only insulted me, you have also ruined the puja." Then she turned to me and said, although for his benefit, "And what did you do anyway that he caught hold of you like this by your hair and dragged you away? Was it that you attended the puja? There were so many other girls there! Does that mean they are all bad? None of *their* husbands complained." Then she added, "Only you can survive with this man. I don't know how you can take all this without complaining. Had it been me I would have taught him a thing or two . . ." And shouting and screaming like this, she left.

I was now worried that he would take all his anger out on me, so I went toward the door and stood in the shadows, hoping he would not see me on his way out. A little while later I saw him going off to work. I knew he'd be furious when he came back, so I quickly fed the children and put them to sleep. When Dulal came in the evening, I told him everything and he also gave me a talking-to. "Why do you go there when you know he doesn't like it?" he asked me. I thought to myself: *It's not as though I went there on my own, there were so many other people there, and even if I had been alone, what was wrong with that?*

I began to think that I would have to do something about my life: things just could not go on like this. My elder son had finished at one school and now needed to move to another, and my younger son had just started school. Money was always needed for little things for them. My husband was reluctant to give money to me, and never without my having to ask at least ten times. I decided that it was time that I looked for work. I started to ask around the neighborhood. I told everyone that I was looking for work. But many just laughed at me. They did not take me seriously. "Why do you need to work?" they asked. "Surely your husband earns enough for all of you?" Someone else said, "You won't be able to work, just forget it." I thought, *If he earns so much, why is there never any money to run the household?*

AND SO LIFE CONTINUED, AND EVERY DAY THERE WAS tension in the home over these things. But I was determined: I had decided that come what may, I would make sure that my children had a good education. I did not want them to be illiterate like their father. I got really furious when my husband asked my elder son to come with him to help push the handcart. The boy would go off with him because his father gave him a little spending money and he could then buy things to eat. And this, too, became a bone of contention. I did not like him giving money to the boy at all. He was getting increasingly spoiled. He'd often skip school and spend the whole day wandering about, and if I said anything to him, his father would tell him to keep quiet and would refuse to speak himself. If, by chance, I raised my hand against the boy, I knew that I would suffer for it at his father's hands. Sometimes the boy would disappear for days on end and then I'd go from place to place hunting for him. At such times my husband put all the blame on me! He was not the least concerned that the boy did not attend school properly, or study. All that was my responsibility. All he did was to give us a little money now and again. I was really at my wits' end. I did not know what to do. My elder son was now in the sixth grade, and we needed money for extra tuition for both him and his younger brother. Their father sometimes gave a little money to the elder boy but he was not at all interested in the younger one. And I was always fearful that their teacher would refuse to teach them.

After years of living with all this, fighting for dignity, for a life for my children, one day I told Shashti's mother that I couldn't take it anymore. She said to me gently, "Child, do you think you can manage to do the kind of work I do?" Would I be able to work in people's houses, to wash their clothes and clean their dishes? I wasn't sure. And what if Baba found out or his friends saw me, what would they say? That Halder's daughter has been reduced to doing this kind of work? When I told Shashti's mother this she said, "If all you are worried about is your father's dignity, then you had better be prepared to suffer and starve." *She's right*, I thought. Why am I so concerned about what Baba will think when he does not seem to be bothered about me at all and hardly ever comes to see me?

Shashti's mother and I were standing by the side of the road talking when an old man, about my father's age, walked up to her and said, "Didi, can you help me to find someone to work in my house?"

"All right, I'll look." Then she looked at me and then back at him and asked him to wait for a minute. She beckoned me to follow her into her house. "Tell me, are you willing to work in his house?"

"Yes, I am," I replied, "but let's at least ask him what kind of work it is."

So we went back to the man and Shashti's mother told him I would work. We went together to his son's house, where I found out that the job entailed doing everything: the cleaning, sweeping, swabbing of the house, washing the clothes, cooking, chopping vegetables, grinding spices . . . I agreed to take it on. That was my first job. I also agreed to the salary his son, Ashish, offered me, as I had no idea what kind of pay to expect.

They seemed to like my work. The family was Brahmin and they held all the customary practices of purity and pollution. But they were quite prepared to let me do everything for them because, after all, they could not do without domestic help. Ashish's wife was somewhat different, wanting to check everything I did, but I did not give her much opportunity because I came to work leaving my small children at home and I was anxious to finish everything quickly and get back to them. Now everyone began talking about what a good worker I was, and suddenly I was in demand. Of course, I could not take on too much. I think perhaps what people liked was that I did not fuss about doing this or that—most girls who were hired preferred to do only specific jobs and weren't prepared to take on everything. Not me. If someone asked me to do something extra, I thought, where's the harm, and I did it. And for this reason I soon found work in several houses and was no longer treated as a servant. My employers became like uncles and aunts to me and their children fondly called me Didi or Pishi.

To manage all the work I now had, each morning, before anyone was awake, I would head off to work and I would finish as much as I could and then return. Then I'd bully and cajole the children to study and start cooking. Then I would send the boys off to school, take my daughter with me, and go off to work again, to return around noon or one. The boys sometimes came home during the break to eat, or else I would take food across to them. Their school finished at four and by the time they came home, I'd have finished everything and would be bathed and dressed. I'd then feed the kids and send them out to play and, while they were playing, cook the evening meal. I'd then send the boys to their tutor, and if sometimes he came to the house instead, I'd make him tea. After all of this was done, I would go out to work again, taking my daughter with me, and in some households they helped to look after her. One young girl would sit my daughter down in her lap and they'd watch television together. I don't think Ashish's wife liked this because she made a barbed comment about it one day: "Amazing," she said, "I've never seen her take my little boy into her lap but to show such love for *your* child . . ." I thought, *Just because we are poor doesn't mean we can't be touched.*

My husband never told me clearly that he did not like me working in other people's homes, so I thought he did not mind. Initially, I even felt a little sorry for him, thinking that perhaps he really was not earning enough to give us money for the household, but then when I looked in his pockets while he was away I found so much money that I got really angry. Then I thought, *Well, it's okay that he has money: after all, it's for the good of the children.* But no sooner had that thought made its presence felt than another followed, and this time I felt resentful, thinking that the least he could have done was to give us enough for our living expenses.

All my earnings went into the house and I did not keep even a single paisa for myself. Then I decided to try to save little bits and pieces and I began to put aside one rupee, two rupees. One day I bought myself a little money box from the market and began to put the money into it. When it filled up, I told Dulal, "Let's break it open!" When we did, we discovered a thousand and fifteen rupees!! I told Dulal I would hide this money away for my daughter. I did not want her father to see it, otherwise he would stop giving even what little he did. I kept it aside and even when times were very hard, I did not touch it. But when it seemed as if I would have to delve into it, because there was a real shortage of money in the home, I gave it to Dulal, saying, "Take it away and do what you like with it." He used the money to purchase gold earrings for my daughter.

I was happy at this, of course, but I wondered when, if ever, my little girl would get the chance to wear the earrings. From the beginning she had been a sickly child, falling ill every now and again, and so she was quite weak. I wanted nothing more than that she should be healthy. I remembered that after I'd come home from hospital with her, I had had to work very hard fetching and carrying water for the house. One day, while feeding at my breast, she caught a terrible chill, and she was so sick that she could hardly breathe. I was really frightened. It was quite late—after nine o'clock on the night of Kali Puja—and her father was not at home. So I picked her up and started to walk out of the house myself. I saw Shashti and her mother standing near their home and talking.

"Where are you taking your little girl at this hour?" Shashti asked.

"Look at her," I said, "she's so sick and I have to take her to a doctor. Her father knows she's ill but he can't be bothered, so what can I do? I have to go alone."

"And where is Dulal?"

"He hasn't come today either."

"Wait a minute and I'll come with you."

There was a doctor near Dulal's house, so I suggested to Shashti that we go there, but by the time we got there the clinic was shut and he had gone. "What shall we do now?" I asked Shashti. Then I suggested we go to Dulal's house and ask his advice. We went there to find he was busy with a puja. He saw us standing there with the girl in my arms, but he paid us no attention. I was really surprised at this and I couldn't say anything. Shashti went up to him and whispered that the child was unwell but even so, he did not seem to be bothered. He just busied himself with whatever he was doing. Finally, I said to Shashti, "Let's go. We'll take her to Dr. Swapan." We walked for about half a mile and finally arrived at his place. By then, it was around ten at night. Dr. Swapan knew my father a little. He took out his stethoscope and listened to the little girl's breathing and then he turned around and scolded me, "Why have you brought her to me when she is already half dead? What am I supposed to do? I will not take a risk. I'll write you a letter and you take her to Dr. Karmakar." The doctor's words filled me with fear. "What will happen to my child, Shashti?" I asked her tearfully.

"Nothing will happen. Just pray to God," she said, "and everything will be all right."

Dr. Swapan pulled out some money and gave it to me. Then he called us a rickshaw and said, "Go on, go to the doctor and make sure you come to see me before you go home."

The rickshaw took us around and around but we couldn't find a doctor's clinic open or find Dr. Karmakar. Finally, he took us to the home of a doctor he knew. It was almost eleven by then. He begged the doctor to examine the child. "Do you have enough money?" the doctor asked. "She needs to be hospitalized."

"Can you not treat her in your home, Doctor?" Shashti asked.

"I'll try," he said, and took her inside.

He had all the facilities in his home, and once inside, he handed the little girl to a nurse and asked her to lay her down on the bed. Then he inserted some kind of tube in her nose. I was watching this fearfully from just outside: I was so scared. I don't know what the doctor put up her nose, or what he pulled out, but the girl started screaming with pain. I could not bear to see her like this and I was clutching Shashti. At that moment, she was the only support I had. Finally, the doctor said I could take her home. He did not charge me too much—perhaps he saw my condition and knew I could not afford it. Even the rickshaw-wallah who was so kind, and took so much trouble, charged me much less than he should have. We were not able to stop by at Dr. Swapan's on the way home because by that time his clinic was closed. The rickshaw-wallah took us all the way home.

When I went in, I found my husband sitting and eating, his face swollen with anger. But the moment he saw the child and the medicines in my hand, his aspect changed. He became really concerned—he must have thought I was out and about with Dulal, which is why he was so angry. The next day Dulal also came in the morning, and I let fly at him unsparingly. He was truly sorry, he took it all, and when I had finished, he accepted that it was his mistake. Then, despite my trying to stop him, he took the girl in his arms and after that day, her care became more or less his sole responsibility.

Once I'd begun to go out to work, it was inevitable that people would stop when they saw me on the road, just for a chat. Someone would ask about my work, someone about home, and we just passed the time talking of this and that. My husband did not like this one bit. Whenever he saw me with someone, he'd wait till I got home and then start abusing me and beating me. If I protested or tried to explain, he'd pick up a large stone and threaten to hurl it at me. He didn't say much about my working outside the house, even though he didn't like it, but if I so much as talked to another man, he would go wild. There was tension if I didn't work and tension if I did—what was I to do? But one day all these worries flew out of my head—albeit for a short while—the day I learned that my mother, my real mother, had come back.

That day I had barely lit the fire to begin cooking after work when my brother's elder daughter, Soma, suddenly came running, jumping from house to house, shouting, "Aunt, Aunt, come quickly! Grandma has come!"

Your grandma has come? So what's so exciting about that? I thought she came over yesterday?"

"Not that grandma!"

"Then which one?"

"My grandma! Come on! Baba has been all over searching for her, and he's finally found out where she's been! Come quick!"

I was stunned. Was it possible? Could it really be my mother? I remembered her face so well. "Let's go," I said to Soma, "let's go and see."

We ran all the way. When we got there, I found my brother sitting in the veranda of the house. "Go in," he said, "see who I have found. All these years Baba hasn't been able to find her, but I've got her for you."

A crowd had collected at the door. Someone said, "Look, your mother has come." Another said, "She looks just like you!" A third said, "Go, run and tell your father." I went in, and the moment I saw her my head started spinning and I fainted to the ground. My sister-in-law sprinkled oil and water on my forehead and sat me up. I began to howl and say to my brother, "Why did you bring her? We were all right without her. We had told everyone our mother was dead. Where was the need to bring her into our lives again?"

She was very different now. She did not even seem to recognize me. A woman from the neighborhood said to her, "Look, here's your daughter. . . ."

"My daughter? Who? Baby?" she asked. "My elder daughter has left us all and gone." I looked at her. I did not think she would stay with us. The people around said to her that now that her elder son had brought her to his home, she should stay with him. She said, "No, I'll stay with my younger son. He lives apart from everyone, I'll be all right with him. Why create a confusion again? I've only come here for a few days, I'll go back there."

My brother asked, "Don't you want to go back to Baba?"

"He has another Ma now, why should I create problems for him?"

Anger, sadness, happiness: didn't she feel any of these at seeing her children after so many years? I didn't see any of these things in Ma. And I think in my heart of hearts, I felt the same. Sometimes there is an expectation, a joy, a soaring, elating feeling in someone's coming home. Nothing like that happened to me. If I felt happiness at all, it was no different from what one feels at meeting a chance acquaintance. Memories came flooding back: some happy, some sad. I wondered again how she could have left such small children and gone away, and in that condition. Did she even remember that she had managed to rid herself of her little girl, Baby, by bribing her with ten paise on the day she left home? Did she remember that she hadn't turned around once to look back? How then could she have known that Baby stood there and watched her until she became a mere speck on the horizon, until the eyes could not see her anymore? Had she turned once and seen her daughter standing there, would she not have come back to embrace her, to take her in her arms and love her . . . ? Perhaps Ma did not even know that that child was now a mother of three.

I looked at her again. She looked ill. She spoke very little. She still had sindoor in her hair, a large *tika* on her forehead. But for whom? For a man who had no time to remember her, who was doing perfectly well without her? I had imagined that when we finally met she would take me in her arms and hold me close, but this Ma did not even seem to know me. I asked her if she got any peace by leaving us and going away, but she did not answer. Then I asked if she remembered that she had pressed ten paise into my hand before she left and she said, "Shut up! Don't talk nonsense!" Did she really not remember any of this? She seemed to me like someone who had suffered a lot. The way she refused to understand what I was saying made me wonder if perhaps she had gone a bit mad.

She stayed with my brother for a month and then she left. Nothing would persuade her to stay longer. We also took her to see Baba. He took one look at her and said, "Where were you all this time? You destroyed my life: why have you come back now?"

"I haven't come to stay. If I hadn't been dragged here by my elder son, I would never have come." Then, after a while, she added, "I am fine staying with my younger son. It's all very well to say I destroyed your life and went away, but what have you done? You earn so much but have you been able to give any of the children a proper upbringing? How did you marry the younger daughter off where you did? You are content to spend all the money on yourself, but you've never thought to give her anything. Who do you think will look after you in your old age? No one. And do you know how far my house is from the office in Kolkata where you used to work? Barely a stone's throw away. If you had wanted, you could have easily found me. But you weren't really interested. How do you think my elder son managed to find me?" The brother with whom my mother now lived had one child. Perhaps this was why she was so anxious to rush back. I wondered: Did she love this one grandchild that much, then?

Before she left, Ma came to visit me as well. Lots of people from around collected to see her. Some of the girls asked if she was my real mother and I said, "Yes, and she's come to see me after twenty years." But I wasn't able to say good-bye to her. I was at work, and by the time I got to my brother's house, I found she had already left. When I asked my brother, he wasn't able to give me a proper address for her. I thought I might go to see her, but no one was willing to take me there, and they kept saying that it would be really difficult to take all the children and go there, so it would be better to forget about it.

I met my mother after so many years, but I couldn't stop her leaving again. A few days after she had gone, my youngest brother came to visit us with his wife. I don't know why, but when I saw him I could not stop the tears. I asked him, "Bhai, do you know who I am?"

"How can I not know you, Didi?" he said. "Can it be that people of the same blood do not know each other?"

"No one has called me Didi before this, Bhai," I said. "Please, can you call me Didi again?" I saw that his eyes welled up with tears, too, though he tried to hide them.

"So, tell me," he said, "how many children do you have?"

"Ma did not want to stay with us," I said as we went in, "she only wants to stay with you."

Two or three days later he left. Then I learned that my elder brother had also moved to Delhi. So now, apart from Baba, there was no one there I could call family. And as for my father, he was as good as not there. At least with my brother I would go across to visit sometimes: now there'd be no one left. No one to turn to in sorrow or joy, no one who could intervene when I got beaten . . . but what could I do? How could I go anywhere with three children in tow? Sometimes when I looked at my husband, I felt a sort of compassion for him. And then I wondered why I could not live the way he wanted me to, be the person he wanted me to be. We had nothing at all in common: perhaps that was the root of all our troubles. I couldn't understand why things were like this for us—there were so many families I knew of where things were well between the husband and wife, where they truly shared a life, where they went out together . . . Many people said of my husband that he was a good man, that he was straight, that he didn't have a bad thought in his heart. Sometimes I also thought that he was a good man, and that perhaps he was unduly influenced by others and they were the ones instigating fights between us. But there were other times when I was unable to bear the way he treated me and I would ask myself, Am I an animal or a human being for him to treat me this way? I remembered how he had behaved with me when I had gone for the puja at Dulal's house. Since that day, I had not wanted to go home to my husband.

The puja used to take place every year at Dulal's home and I used to help with the arrangements—making sure everything was in the right place. I also helped with the decorations—not only there but in other homes as well. In fact, whenever there was a puja, a marriage, or some sort of function in the neighborhood, people would call me to do the floor designs, the *alpana*, and the decorations. I enjoyed this very much.

On the day of the puja, I fasted and waited at home for my husband to return from work. I had put together some things for the puja—fruit, some food, a conch shell, a small stool. It was around two in the afternoon. Normally, my husband would come back by that time but that day, it was close to evening and there was no news of him. I thought he must have gotten delayed at work. I was waiting because when he came, I would give him his food and then I could go to the puja. It was well after five when he came. I served him his dinner and when he had finished, I told him I was going to the puja. He asked, "How late will you be?"

"I'll be back as soon as it's over," I said. He did not say anything, so I left. Everyone there was waiting for me. I did everything I had to do, cut up the fruit and so on, and then it was time to go to the pond to fetch water. Dulal, the Brahmin priest, I, and several others, as well as the musicians and drummers, all went to the pond. I was the only woman there. That was my mistake, and I had to pay for it. My husband saw me going alone with the men to the pond. He came and disrupted the puja and shouted the vilest of abuses at me. Then he began to beat me up. Everyone watched. Dulal and Ravi-da's wife came and dragged me away, and she took me upstairs to her home. That night I decided I would not go back. Ravi-da's wife tried all kinds of arguments to explain to me why I had to go back, but I was now determined. I refused to listen. I spent the night there. My husband kept hanging around the house for hours and once he even came inside. Ravi-da's wife explained things to him and sent him away. Then she tried to talk me around, but I told her, "I'm not going there anymore. Only I know what I have had to bear living with him, now I've had enough. If I go back, the same thing will start all over again and my life will not only be a living hell but it will become a sideshow for anyone who wants to watch."

In the morning my elder son came with a small box in which he had packed clothes for himself and his younger brother and sister. I told him, "Son, you stay with your father. I am going to your grandfather's house. Come and see me there so I can get news of you." And with that, I left for Baba's house. When my husband got to know that my son had brought our clothes to us, he was furious. He beat the boy up and then threw him out of the house. My son came to me crying and told me the whole story. I told him not to worry, that he should come and stay with me, and I would work hard to make a life for all of us.

Perhaps my father thought this time would be like all the

others, when I would stay for a few days until my anger had cooled and then return. But when he saw that I was determined not to go back, he did not know what to do. Tensions began to build up between him and Ma. I knew that I would have to do something and quickly, otherwise my presence and that of my three children would only make things worse between the two of them. And I could not expect them to feed us. So one day I went to see Shashti. She took me to a hospital in search of work. There, we were told that we could come back after two weeks and start work. I wondered, Would I be able to do that sort of filthy work? But then I thought of the children and realized I had to do it. I went home and told Baba that I would take a separate place on rent and live there.

"But how will you pay the rent?" Baba asked me. I thought, *He's right, how will I pay?* I had not a paisa with me at the time. Still, I asked Dulal also if he could find me a place to live, thinking that once I began to work in the hospital I would have money to pay the rent. Two days later he found me a house and I moved in. In the hospital, too, everything was settled about who would work when: Shashti was given morning duty and I had to work nights. I had to leave my young children at home and go to work. Now and again, I would go to Baba's and get some money for my day-to-day expenses, and this led to many fights between him and Ma.

Despite the fact that I was now living alone, Baba still thought I would go back to my husband. He kept insisting I should go back and I kept insisting that I would not. I told him I wanted to live on my own now, I wanted to see if I could manage to feed and look after my children. I did not go back to him, but one day Vibhu-da brought Shankar to my home. Perhaps they thought they could take me back. I was sitting outside my door with the children when I saw Vibhu-da and my husband coming down the road. I continued to sit there. Vibhu-da came and stood in front of me on the veranda and said, "Come home."

"No, Dada," I replied, "I will not go there anymore. He is okay on his own, let him be like that." After this I did not speak and whatever was said was spoken by Vibhu-da. My husband only spoke up when one of the neighbors said to him, "So, Brother, you've come to take your wife away?"

"Is she a cow or a goat that I can take her away?" he snapped back.

"Then have you come to see that your cow-goat is living all right? Is that why you have come?" she asked.

As soon as she'd said this, Vibhu-da told my husband they should leave and they did. I would not go with him then, nor ever. People often said to me that if I didn't go back, I'd face the consequences later, but what do they mean by "later"? After all, there are women without husbands who get on with their lives, aren't there? Don't their days pass well? Then there were others, among whom I count my father, who insisted that if I lived alone that would be disastrous for my children's education. To them my answer was: I'll see to it that they study. I thought to myself that it is only because of me that my elder son has studied the little that he has; and that I've managed alongside looking after two small children, working, running the home . . . The worst thing that could happen would be that my workload would increase a bit. Nothing more.

After working for a while at the hospital I began to feel that perhaps it was not a good idea to leave the children alone at night. So I left that job. Then, when things became difficult again, I went to Baba's house. There, Baba and I fought so much about my husband that he shouted at me, "If you don't want to go back to him, then get out of here!" The next day I asked him gently, "Baba, can you give me my brother and sister-in-law's

address? And if you give me a little money, I will go there." Baba
agreed.

My train was at two o'clock the next day. I was restless from
the morning. I did not change the children's clothes or mine, and
with Baba, Ma, and Patit Kaku, I went to the station. Dulal also
came to see us off. Baba handed the ticket to me. My eyes welled
up with tears. I don't know what kinds of thoughts and fears were
going around in my head, but I found myself crying and sobbing.
Baba was sad, because now he would not have any of his children
close to him. I was also thinking of my husband, and many things
I would have liked to have said to him went through my mind. I
was finding it difficult to go away, to leave him behind.

Baba looked at me and said, "Why are you crying, child? You
can go back to him even now. So what if I lose the money for the
ticket? Just go." But I did not listen to him. It was time for the
train. Baba wrote down my brother's address in Faridabad on a
piece of paper. I told Dulal, "Look after yourself." He took my
daughter in his arms and held her. I thought, *Why can't my father
hold me in this way and show me just a little love? I know he is sad at
my going. Could it be that he does not want to do this because of Ma?*

I was thinking all these thoughts when the train drew in. I
touched everyone's feet, took Dulal's hand, and then took my
children and climbed onto the train. The train moved away and
I waved to everyone with tears in my eyes. I was saying good-bye.

The carriage was so crowded there wasn't even room to stand,
let alone for three children to sit. I told my elder son, Babu, to
keep hold of his younger brother and sister and to stand to one
side while I looked for a place to sit. Then somehow I managed to
squeeze out a space on the floor where I put our bags. I got hold of
the children and we all just parked ourselves on top of the bags.
The children were delighted at the prospect of traveling by train,
but my heart was heavy with worry: Would we ever be able to re-

turn, I wondered. I was leaving everything behind, and who knew what awaited me in the future? Would I be able to look after these children? To bring them up properly? Night fell as my thoughts wandered here and there. I told the children to put their heads in my lap and try to sleep. The two little ones went off to sleep quickly, but my elder son's eyes stayed wide open. He looked at me and said, "Ma, why don't you try to sleep a little?"

I said, "No, child, I'm not sleepy at all. I'm just worried. I'm doing this for you children, and yet I have no idea what awaits us. Will I be able to look after you?"

He said, "But I'm also going to work and so are you, so what's there to worry about? And your brothers, our mamas, are there as well . . ."

"Yes, but how long will they look after us? In the end, we'll have to fend for ourselves. Anyway, let's just see what happens."

"Ma," he said, "the little ones will have to go to school, they must study. As for me, it doesn't matter . . ." But I felt that it *did* matter: he wanted to study and learn. I so wanted for him to be able to do so. But that did not happen. What could I do? Some of the responsibility lay with him, but mostly it was because of his father. After all, shouldn't a father take care of his children? It's not enough just to have money, you have to also take responsibility for it. Is it fair that I should shout myself hoarse, while you just stand by and watch? I try my best to turn our child into a responsible person, and you, you spoil him by throwing money his way occasionally? This is why his studies came to a standstill.

These thoughts went round and round in my head and before I knew it, it was morning. The conductor came round and I showed him our tickets. "Why did you get into this compartment?" he demanded. He wrote something on a piece of paper and then said, "You'll have to pay one hundred and seventy-five rupees extra." I had bought our tickets before boarding the train, so why was he asking for money again? But then I thought, I may as well give it to him: I have money right now, so it's best to give it, for who knows what he may do, especially since the children are with me.

Some time later another conductor came, and the same thing started all over again. I felt really terrible. I thought, *If all the money goes on this, how will I be able to feed the children?* I began to cry. When the children saw me weeping, they began to cry as well. The conductor then said, "You'd better keep the money ready. I'll be back shortly."

Another passenger, a Bengali, asked my elder son what had happened and the boy told him the whole story. So he said, "All right, let the fellow come back and we will see. We'll explain things to him and he will not ask for money again." Suddenly I felt I was able to breathe again. But thankfully, the conductor never came back. As the train was nearing Delhi, the Bengali gentleman asked us where we planned to go. "Is there anyone else with you?" he asked. My son answered all his questions and started telling him everything about us. I was worried in case he reported us or did something to us. I kept the children close to me. Then the gentleman said to me as he gathered up his things, "Look, this is a new place, and you must be careful. Make sure you keep your children with you at all times."

Finally, the train drew into the Delhi railway station. I was clutching the piece of paper with the address Baba had given me in my hand as we got off the train. We had to find out where to get the train to Faridabad, so I began to ask around. "Faridabad? What Faridabad?" said someone. My heart filled with fear. Had Baba given me the wrong address? Where had I come? What would I do now? Where would I go with the children? Then I thought I'd ask the coolies. I asked one: he knew nothing. He asked another man who told us in Hindi that the train for Faridabad would not leave from that platform but from another one. I took the children and, still clutching my piece of paper, we crossed over to the other platform, all the while asking people.

Once there, we waited for the train, which soon arrived. I asked my elder son to take the bag of clothes and I picked up my daughter, held the small boy by his hand, and we pushed our way into the train. Three or four stations later, when the train stopped again, I checked with another woman if this was Faridabad. She said it was, so I quickly grabbed the children and our bags, and got off the train.

I had a piece of paper with me with the address of my brother on it. I showed it to the rickshaw-wallah and I asked him how far it was. He said, "Sit, I'll take you there." He dropped us off near a Hanuman mandir. I made the children sit in a shop nearby and set off, asking passersby, in Hindi, if they knew my brother or where he lived. But nobody seemed to know, and once again I began to worry: What had I done?

Gradually people started to collect around me. One woman said to me in Hindi, "Don't be frightened, sister, we are also outsiders here. If you don't find anyone else, we are here for you." A Punjabi woman came up to me and said, "Come home with me. The children must be hungry—I'll cook something and you can feed them." Just then another man came and pointed to a nearby hill. "There is a Bengali settlement just over there," he said. "Perhaps you'll find your brother there?"

I went there and looked around. There was a small temple and behind it, a little cluster of houses grouped together in a basti. I left the children on the steps of the temple and went into the basti. I asked around, but no one seemed to know my brothers. I saw some people playing cards near the temple and I went and asked them. A young boy jumped up and said, "You mean the man who drives a car?"

I said, "Brother, can you tell me his name, please?"

He gave me the correct names of my brothers and I heaved a sigh of relief. I asked him to tell me where they were. But he said they were not there anymore, that they had left some time ago. Then he mentioned a man named Vimal who would know how to find them. "He is the one who taught your brother how to drive," he said, "he'll surely know where he is." I asked if he would be kind enough to take me to Vimal's house, but when we arrived, we discovered that Vimal was away at work. We met his wife and she was kind and offered us lunch.

When Vimal came back that evening, I asked him about my brothers. He said, "Oh, they are in Chakkarpur now. The bus fare there costs twenty or twenty-five rupees or so."

I said to him, "Please come with me, Vimal-da. You can just drop me there and come straight back."

He replied that he wouldn't be able to come with me right then. "But you know you have a cousin here. Your mother's sister's daughter . . ."

"A cousin? My aunt's daughter? Which one?"

"Why, don't you remember your Badi-budi?"

"Of course! Oh, please show me where she lives."

I thought, *Thank heavens I have found someone from my family after all!* But on the heels of this thought came another: I had already fought with Badi-budi once. Who knows whether she would even be willing to talk to me? But nonetheless, I went along to her home with Vimal-da.

She was sitting in the veranda making rotis. Vimal-da called out, "Hey, Budi! Just turn around and see who has come to see you." For a moment, I panicked. What would I do if she refused to talk to me? But the minute she set eyes on me, she broke into a smile and greeted me so warmly that I knew she had forgotten our little fight. "What are you doing standing there, Didi?" she said to me, "Come in, come in! Have you fought with Brother-in-law?"

"Yes," I said, "something like that."

"But how did he let you come away?"

"Leave it be . . . do you really think he could stop me once I'd made up my mind to go? Of course, when he finds out he'll kick up a fuss. But never mind that: tell me, where are Dada and the others? Where do they stay? Can I go to them now?"

"At this time? Forget it. Stay over and start out in the morning. After breakfast, I'll take you there myself. But how do you plan to stay there with these children?"

"Why shouldn't I be able to? I'm not going to live off my brothers. I'll find a job . . ."

"Work should not be a problem—there are a lot of women working there. So many women who are alone, separated from their husbands, trying to earn a living . . . you'll certainly find work, but the problem is that the moment you do, you'll have to move out of your brothers' home and take a place on rent."

Vimal-da got up and said he had to leave. I asked him if he thought it would be possible for me to get work there. He said yes, it would, and if I didn't, I should come straight back here. And then he left.

No sooner had he gone than Badi-budi turned to me and said, "So what did you fight about so much that you had to leave Durgapur?" I told her everything clearly.

"I'm surprised that you have managed to come so far with three children and all this baggage. How did you cope?"

"Why, what is so difficult about this? Don't you know that if you have an address or a place to go, you can travel great distances to find it?"

The next morning I woke up the children and fed and bathed

them properly—they had not had a bath or a good meal for two whole days. It was two o'clock before we managed to set off. We took a rickshaw to the bus stop. Badi-budi's husband saw us to the bus, and told the driver to put us down at the Chakkarpur turning. When we reached our stop, we got off the bus and started walking. A short distance down the road, we saw my elder sister-in-law and her daughter washing their feet outside their home.

"Look, there's your sister-in-law," said Badi-budi. When I got closer I saw how pale and thin she had become. And she barely talked to me. I looked at Badi-budi. She understood immediately what I wanted to say and before I could open my mouth she said, "Look, if you stay here with them, you will be very unhappy. You will not be able to bear it. You'll have to listen to everything they say. Just remember, the moment you get a job, you must find yourself a small place to live and move out. Stay here only as long as is necessary—you don't have much choice." I thought how right she was: I knew that was exactly what would happen. "But what if I don't find work here?" I asked.

"No, there's no question of not finding work. You'll find something. You just have to look around a bit."

My younger brother's home was close to my elder brother's. I went with Budi to his home but here, too, I faced the same reaction: my sister-in-law took one look at me and turned her face away. I had come from so far away and rather than making me feel welcome, my sisters in-law were behaving as if I were a great burden on them. I asked Budi, "Well, do you think I will be able to live here at all? From the looks of it, I think that perhaps I should leave right away . . ."

The next morning Budi got ready to leave. Now there was no one even to talk to me politely in my brothers' homes. Budi reminded me before leaving, "Just remember: if you don't find work here, come to me. I'm always there."

I felt a little heartened. I thought that if I needed to go away, at least I had her home to escape to—and who knows? I might even find work there.

Budi left and I returned to my brother's home. My younger brother seemed to be a little better off than my elder brother—he worked as a driver and earned a reasonable income. I had thought that I might stay with him for a few days, but his wife was so unwelcoming that I did not want to go there. But my older brother had only one room in which he lived with his wife and his four daughters. How could my children and I share such a small space?

I was mulling this all over when my brother and Ratan arrived. Ratan's sister was married to my younger brother. He also lived in Durgapur, and when my Baba had learned that Ratan was in search of work, he'd suggested that he take me with him to Chakkarpur where he was planning to go. At that time, Ratan had agreed, so when I saw him I asked him, "Hey, Ratan, when did you come here?" He said that he'd only been there a few days.

"But you were going to bring me with you. What happened?"

"What could I do?" he said. "Everyone there told me not to."

The moment my brother heard this, he started berating me. "Why did you leave everything and come here? If you had to come, at least you should have brought Shankar with you. Ratan has been with me for a while, and now you, with your children . . . ? How am I going to keep you all here?"

I did not say a word to him. I knew that if I said anything he would be furious. Finally, he calmed down. Soon afterward, a young man he knew came to visit. His name was Subhash and he lived close by in a rented room. Suddenly, while talking to him, my brother turned to me and said, "*Arre*, Baby, I completely forgot! I have another room, and I'm paying rent on it for nothing. I had planned to open a shop there. Why don't you move in there? You could stay till you find work and if Ratan wants, he can also stay there with you."

I looked at Ratan. I could see that the idea appealed to him. My brother realized that we were both happy with this arrangement. So then he told his friend Subhash, "You know, Subhash, you are cooking for yourself right now. Why don't you hand over your pots and pans to Baby and she can cook for you alongside her own family? Right now she has a few constraints as well, so your pots and pans will come in handy, and you could pay her whatever you spend on your food. Once she finds work she can return your things." Subhash thought this was an excellent suggestion and the arrangement was finalized.

Still, it took some days to leave my brother's home. I got the pots and pans from Subhash's home, but it took time to clean up the new place and to set everything as I wanted it to be. It was difficult to find the time to do this, as the whole day was spent out on the streets, going from house to house in search of work, and worrying about how to feed the children. In the evenings, when I came back, I would go either to my elder brother's place or to my younger brother's to eat. But it was not a nice feeling: when no one talks to you properly, there's no pleasure in their company. The thing that made me happiest was the thought that once I'd moved into my new place, I would only have to meet my sisters-in-law when I wanted to!

BEING IN MY OWN PLACE MEANT MORE WORK, BUT IT also meant more money. Subhash and Ratan paid me twenty rupees each every day, and every now and again my brother would slip me some money without telling anyone. I would cook for everyone in the morning and would then set out to look for work, but everywhere I went, the same question kept coming up: "Where is your husband?" The moment I said that he was not with me, that he lived in the village, the prospect of a job would disappear.

I spent many hours and many days in search of work, but everywhere I met with the same resistance. I began to worry about what would become of us. I was really scared that I would have to return to my husband.

My elder brother also asked around a lot but was not able to find a job for me. Then one day he said to me, "Why don't you go back and bring Shankar with you?" And I thought, if this was what I had to do, I may as well have stayed there with him. Surely, I hadn't traveled all this way, and gone to all this trouble, just to go back to where I'd started? Every now and again my sister-in-law would raise the same question with me and with my younger brother and his wife. It was as if they had learned a lesson by heart, the way they kept impressing on me again and again that I should not have left him. All of them thought that it would have been better for me to die than leave the home of my swami, my lord and master. No one so much as tried to understand why I had left. More than anything, I wanted that my children should have a good life. It is not enough to give birth, for birth brings with it a responsibility: the responsibility to enable a person to grow into a human being. My husband could not—or did not want to—understand this. For if he had, it would also have meant sharing that responsibility, and he was not interested in that. This also means providing a good atmosphere and surroundings, but he did not want to change our situtation, and we used to fight about this in front of the children. It was that that made me realize that things would not work out and that I had to be strong and find a way out of this mess.

So I thought, *Well, if people think I'm doing the wrong thing, let them*. I'll just keep on looking for work and someday, somehow, I'll find it. There were so many working people living in that area, surely I wasn't going to be the only one without a job? I *would* find work: I was determined to.

One day my younger brother and I were arguing about this when a friend of my elder brother's, Nitai, arrived. When he heard about my situation and how I had been going from pillar to post in search of work, he said, "Don't worry, Didi, leave it to me. I'll find some work for you." Meanwhile, my elder brother had been looking as well, and one day my sister-in-law took me to a large house close by. She had talked to the owners about giving me some work, and once there, she explained everything to me. So I finally found my first job.

But barely a few days had passed before people around started to say, "Oh, so you're working in *that* house, eh? But they are very bad people and they don't pay well. In fact they try to get out of paying at all . . . and they're very difficult people to work for." People said all kinds of things but I refused to pay them any heed and carried on working. I thought that it had taken me so long to find anything, and work was so hard to come by, and now that I had my first job, it would be foolish of me to just listen to what people were saying and let go without even trying! Surely they would pay me at the end of the month? But I'd barely been working there a week when one day Nitai suddenly showed up and said, "Didi, I have found work for you in a large house. You had better come with me and see what you have to do." So I went off with him straightaway.

On the way I asked if the people he had found would give me a place to stay. He said he had mentioned it to them but that I should discuss it with them myself. When we got there, I waited outside while Nitai rang the bell. A woman came out. She seemed really nice, at least in appearance. Nitai talked to her while I waited quietly. After a while she asked me, "Will you be able to work from eight in the morning to seven at night?"

"Yes," I replied, "but if I could get a small place to stay that would be very good, because otherwise I will have to leave my children on their own the whole day. If you can give me a place to stay, I will work night and day for you."

It was settled that I would come back the next morning at eight. I went immediately to the house I'd been working in and told them I would be leaving, but a couple of hours later, Nitai came back and told me that it would be better if I waited a bit. "Those people say they'll take you on after a few days," he said.

I was in total shock! What had I done? Why had I been so foolish, so precipitate? On his advice I'd given up even what I had, and what would my brother and sister-in-law say when they heard? The memsahib in whose house I had worked for a few days came to see me and took me to her house again. "Look," she said, "if you don't come back to work for me, I will not pay you for those few days you have worked there." So I thought, *Well, let her not pay me.* And once again I came away from her house.

I'd listened to Nitai and left my job immediately, but then, I reasoned with myself, that was not his fault. After all, he only passed on what those people had said to him. The fault lay with me, for without firming up things with my new employer, I'd let go of the old job. What could I do now? I thought I should go back to the place Nitai had taken me and ask them directly about when I should begin work. So I went there and rang the bell and immediately a young boy of sixteen or seventeen came out. I asked him to call the memsahib, and when she came out, her face fell. She said, "Oh, it's you again is it? Why have you come back? I told Nitai I would send word if I needed you."

I said, "Look, after finalizing things with you, I've left my other job. What should I do now, tell me? It's so difficult to find work."

"All right, wait here. Let me see what I can do." She went inside and came out with some rice and a little money, which she offered me. "Take this," she said, "and feed your children and I will send you word through Nitai when I need you."

I took the rice and money and went to Nitai, who worked as a caretaker in a house nearby. At the time, his employers, the sahib and memsahib, were not home. I went and rang the bell and he leaned out of the third floor to ask who it was. When he saw me, he came and opened the door. Before I could say anything, he pulled me inside. There I found my brother and his wife, who looked surprised to see me. My sister-in-law would not even speak to me properly, but even so, I asked when they had come there. They did not answer me, but Nitai said they'd come to visit and he'd persuaded them to stay. My instinct was to run away, since they were being so cold to me, but Nitai kept insisting I stay. The more he insisted, the more my brother was displeased, but Nitai did not let me go until he had fed all of us.

After I had left, my brother and Nitai had words about my coming there. Nitai told my brother, "She is your own sister—and she is like a sister to me as well. Look at how she's having to run around in search of work. Things are so difficult for her, but you people are not doing a thing for her. She came to me in search of work and I talked to the people next door, and that is why she came here, to tell me what had happened. If you can come to my home, what is the problem with your sister coming to my home?" And to this my brother, my real, blood brother, replied: "If she comes to see you, I will break my friendship with you."

Nitai told me all this later. I was not surprised. In fact, I had warned Nitai when I was leaving his home that he could expect my brother to say something unpleasant about my coming to see him. And I thought to myself, *If this is what my own brother thinks of me, why should I be surprised at what others say?*

The following day, I went to Nitai to ask if the people in the house next door had said anything to him yet. Nitai said, "Are they still giving you the runaround? How are you managing to feed the children?" He knew very well how my brother treated me. "Wait here. I'll go and check with them." And leaving me there, he went to see the memsahib.

I learned later that he asked her why she did not give me a clear answer. "Why don't you just tell her whether you want her to work or not? What's the point in keeping her hanging?" The memsahib did not get angry at this at all. She said to him, "All right, son, I'll let you know by tomorrow morning." She kept me waiting like this for another week or ten days and then suddenly, one afternoon, without warning, she came to Nitai and said, "Go and get her quickly. Tell her if she wants to work here she'd better come at once." So Nitai rushed to find me, and said, "Come quickly! She's calling you." I went at around four or five in the afternoon and she kept me there till eight. I was worried that I had left my children without telling them anything. Around eight o'clock, the memsahib came and said to me, "I can give you a place to stay but not straightaway. It will take some time, but I'll let you know. For the moment, you will have to come like this every day and work." I had no choice in the matter, so I agreed.

The next day, I got to work around eight in the morning. I saw then that I was one of four people working there and my job was to work inside the house. They seemed to like my work a great deal. There was another girl like me working there, and in the beginning, she would not talk to me because she did not realize I was a Bengali. One day I spoke to her in Hindi and asked her where her home was. When she said Kolkata, I spoke to her in Bengali, and asked if she was Bengali. She was quite taken aback and looked at me in surprise. "I'm Bengali, too," I explained, "and we can talk to each other in our own language." But the owners did not like their servants talking to each other. If they saw their servants sitting, standing, or just talking, they would immediately pull them up. The Bengali girl was happy that I was from the same place and she told me that she felt reassured now that she knew where I was from. "I've been quite lonely," she said, "and it's nice to know there is someone I can talk to, but our mistress does not like us talking to each other, so what can we do?" I thought, *Well, there's nothing much we* can *do.* I had no alternatives. I needed the job, so I would have stayed on whatever the conditions. I had nowhere else to go.

Barely had a few days gone by when one day the memsahib called out to me, "Baby, come here." I hurried to her, worried that something had happened for her to call out to me like that. "Go and pack your belongings," she said, "and get your children and come here." But how could I do that? Just pack up everything on their say-so and bring it all there? Apart from anything, I would have to bathe the children, wash and dry the clothes . . . so I said to her, "I can't manage this today. I will come after two days. I've lived with discomfort for so many days, a few more won't matter. I'll finish everything that needs to be done in the house and get the children's hair cut and do all the other things I need to do." But this made the memsahib very angry. "When you did not have a place to stay you were begging for one, and now that I am giving you one, you don't seem to want it!" Why should I object? What could be better for me? I wondered. At the moment, I have to leave my small children behind and come this far to work and who knows what they have to listen to in my absence. Then when I get back after work, they come running to me, crying out "Ma, Ma!" in such pathetic voices that I feel terrible, and every day they ask me why I am so late. How can I tell them that if you are working for someone else, you can only be free when they give you their permission?

But the memsahib was not mollified. So I said, "All right. I'll go tonight and fetch my children and bring everything."

"Not tonight, go right *now*. Leave aside what you are doing and bring your things right away."

I did as I was told and quickly made my way home. My elder brother saw me and was surprised. "So early today? Is something wrong?"

"I've come to fetch the children," I said. "The memsahib has told me to bring everything at once . . ."

"Go, go!" he said "That's excellent. Go quickly."

I thought, *They'll all be relieved to see me go.* My brother had found my elder son a job in some house, but he hadn't told me where it was and I had no idea how to find him. So I asked him to keep an eye out for him and I collected my things, took my younger son and my daughter with me, and rushed back to the memsahib's house. By the time we arrived, it was around eight or nine at night. I rang the bell and the memsahib and the Bengali servant girl came out at once. The memsahib said, "What took you so long? Go now, go and sleep. There's no need to do any work right now." I thought, *She hasn't even asked if we have eaten anything or not.* Luckily I had bought the children some things to eat from the shop because I thought there wouldn't be time to cook.

We managed to get through the night somehow. From the next day, the burden of work increased so much that sometimes I barely had time to breathe. I couldn't understand why, but people were always after me: do this, do that, there's work to be done here, and here . . . and because they had given me a place to stay, I couldn't even say anything. Sometimes I did not even have the time to cook proper food for the children, and no one seemed to be concerned. Often I'd be working till eleven at night and there was no concern that my children might be hungry or that

I needed to go and check on them. So I had to cook for the next day before I went to bed at night and this would often mean that it would get very late. In the morning I had to be up before six—memsahib called for me every morning. I'm a light sleeper, so I'd wake at the first call but even so, she'd keep calling out until she saw me.

Memsahib's daughter worked in an office in Delhi and had to leave home by eight, before which I had to get her breakfast ready. In the evenings, she came back around six. I was required to wait at the gate for her bus to arrive and as soon as she got down, I'd take her bag and anything else she had and walk her into the house. Some days, if I was late, I would get a shouting. I also had to keep some fruit ready for her to eat, and as soon as she sat down I'd offer her tea, water, sherbet, whatever she wanted. Then, if she wanted, I had to massage her head or her feet or whatever: the work was never-ending.

Sometimes the sahib told his wife, "Look, this girl also needs some rest. Why don't you give her a bit of time off? I'm sure she'd like to spend a little time with her children . . ." But his wife did not like this. I could understand all this, but I kept my silence—after all, I had my children. If she threw me out where would I go? There was no way I could live with my brothers, but I couldn't manage without going to their homes, either, because that was the only way I could get news of my elder son—and then there was my memsahib, who would not let me go anywhere. If I ever asked her if I could go and get some news about my son, she'd say no, not right now, there's too much work. If I said I had to go and buy provisions, she'd tell me to go and come back by a certain time. If I was late she would shout at me. I wasn't allowed to go anywhere, or to talk to anyone. It was really difficult to stay there like this. But I did not know anyone whom I could ask to help me find some other work. There were other people working in that house, but somehow she did not get at them in quite the same way as she did with me. I was the one who was made to work the hardest—perhaps she thought that since she had given me room to live with my children, she had a greater claim on my time.

In some ways, things were not so bad. I lived in a large house. We ate reasonably well. I was getting paid regularly, and I had even managed to save a little bit. But I missed my son, and often I would just sit and weep thinking of him. The Bengali girl encouraged me to ask our memsahib for time off to go and look for my son. "Go on, ask her," she said, "what's the use of crying like this? I don't know how you cope, not knowing what has happened to your son." *Yes*, I thought, *only I knew how I was managing.*

One day, on the way back from the market, I decided to go to my brother's house. My son was sitting outside. It was terrible. He seemed to have all kinds of cuts and bruises on his hands and feet and he couldn't walk properly. His foot was bleeding. I was so upset to see him, I wondered if he even got fed where he was working. I decided to take him to the doctor—my brother saw him as I was leaving and came and said, "Why don't you send the boy home? If you don't want to go back don't go, but send the boy back to his father. Or else, take him away from here."

I said, "Brother, I live in someone's house. I already have two children with me there. They won't let me have another child with me. Please let him stay on with you for a while until I can find another job or a house and I will come back and take him away." Then I turned to leave.

Back at the house, memsahib gave me job after job: do this, no, do that, finish this first . . . I realized that she was annoyed with me for being late. Finally she asked, "Why were you so late?" So I told her. "I stopped by at my brother's house. I wanted to see my son. He's not well and I had to take him to the doctor. I will go again tomorrow."

She was furious. "Yes, yes, go. Go every day, why don't you? Leave your work and go off, wander about outside."

I thought, *I had hardly been wandering about—when had I ever had a chance to even take a leisurely walk?* I did not like her attitude to me at all. She wouldn't let me go to see my son, and if ever he came to the house to see me, she would not let him enter. I had to go outside to speak to him and even that was only allowed for a limited period of time. I was starved for my son, and I thought, surely he wanted sometimes to talk to his mother and his brother and sister? My Bengali friend sympathized with me, and she encouraged me to leave and look for another job. How will you manage like this? she kept asking me. And she was right, concern for my son was killing me. I was worried about what he was eating, how he was living . . . and because of this I couldn't eat properly, either. My heart wasn't in my work . . . and I had to listen to recriminations all the time.

The family I worked with had a dog called Kesfo. He gave me much more love and attention than that family ever did. When I was sad, he would come and cuddle up to me, lick my feet, nuzzle me with his nose. He understood my sadness. And if I responded by stroking him a little, his tail would begin to wag. Soon we became such good friends that he refused to be looked after by anyone else. I was the one who had to feed him—he would refuse to eat if someone else got his food. I had to take him out for a walk so he could relieve himself. And if I left my door open, he would run into my room, jump on my bed, and settle down there. If I was asleep, he would try to wake me and I understood that he needed to go out. I was also happy to take him out, for when I went out with him, I felt completely safe: no one dared to trouble me whether it was morning or night when I was with him.

Memsahib and sahib often went out and came back very late, sometimes around two or three in the morning, and I had to stay

awake for them and let them in when they came. The other servants, including the Bengali girl, Anjali, were usually asleep by
this time. Anjali and the cook, Bhajan, had an odd relationship.
Suddenly she would stop talking to him, and he would come
to me and say, "Baby, tell her to speak to me." They'd fight and
bicker all the time, and then they'd come running to me for help.
But if I tried to tell them not to fight, it made no difference. All
this came to an end the day Bhajan heard that his mother was very
ill. He had a letter from his father and was so upset to hear about
his mother that he began to cry. He told me his news, and also
that he had asked memsahib to give him some time off so he could
go and see his mother and she had refused. I felt very sorry for
him. "Go and show her the letter," I urged him, "it may help to
change her mind." Instead, he showed the letter to the sahib
and he agreed to give him time off. Sahib treated us much better
than memsahib, and sometimes when she was angry with me, he
would step in and placate her.

The next day Bhajan got ready to go home. He was only waiting to get paid, but our employers were not very forthcoming
with his salary and once again he began to cry. At around two
o'clock, the sahib came and talked to him and asked if Bhajan
would give him an assurance that he would return. Bhajan said he
would go home and see how things were and would then phone
them. So sahib gave him the money he was owed, plus some extra,
and told him that if he came back in a month, he would also get
paid for that month. As he was leaving, Anjali and I advised him
to make sure he came back within a month. And then our sahib
drove him to the train station.

Anjali and I were the only ones left in that house now. *They
will all go away and I will be the only one left*, I thought. But then,
I don't have anywhere to go either. Who can I ask to find me another job? Anjali said, "Why don't you ask Nitai? At least try to

talk to him once." After a couple of days I did, but I got the sense that he had lost interest in trying to help me any further. Also, he was married now and was living in his in-laws' home. I had gotten to know a few of the people working in other places nearby, so I thought I would ask if any of them could find me another job.

One day, Anjali went to Delhi with memsahib. They went to the office through which memsahib had located and employed Anjali. There were some people there from Anjali's village who had originally suggested her to memsahib. When she'd been employed, it had been agreed that she would get two days off a month, when she would be able to go back to this office to spend time with her people. That day, the moment she got a chance, Anjali began to complain and told the people in the office all sorts of things about our memsahib—how she felt the memsahib had no kindness in her soul and thought that if she paid you to work, she owned you: all this and more. Memsahib did not utter a word and despite this she kept Anjali on, perhaps because not many workers stayed long in her home. But then who would, given the way she treated them?

The next time she took Anjali there, Anjali did not return.

One day memsahib brought another woman to work in the house—she was a good worker, but she spoke only Bengali, no Hindi, so she couldn't understand what memsahib said to her, so I had to serve as a translator between the two of them. In this interim, Bhajan came back and took over the work in the kitchen, along with many other responsibilities. Now, suddenly, she began to turn on me: I became the bad one. Nothing I did would please her, and she'd criticize everything . . . she even began to shout at my children. The poor little things, they were locked up on the roof of the house all day and would die to see me just the same way as all the time I was dying to see them. Sometimes they'd come down the stairs and wait for me, but if the memsahib or her daughter saw them, they'd shout at them and shoo them away. The other girl who was working there kept telling me I should find work elsewhere. "Why do you continue to stand for this?" she asked me. I also began to think that if I moved out of that house, at least my children would be able to breathe the air of the outside world.

So one day I took my children and left. I did not ask memsahib or wait for her permission, or take my things. I just left. The only thought in my mind as I left was that I had enough money with me to last us two months and during that time I would find work somewhere else.

A COUPLE OF DAYS LATER, MY ELDER SON AND I WENT and put a deposit on a room. It was in an area where there were no other Bengalis. The rent was a thousand rupees a month, and we paid some of it—I thought at least we would have a place to stay for the time being: then I would look around for something else. I left the children with the Bengali woman who was working in memsahib's house—she lived in her own home—and I took a rickshaw to go and collect my things. I went to the house and rang the bell, and the dog started barking and came running out. I stroked his head through the bars of the gate and we waited. In a short while sahib came and opened the gate. The dog jumped up at me and began whimpering. I felt terrible: I'd only been gone two days and this was how he felt. What would happen to him when I went away for good?

I was a little nervous about telling memsahib that I was leaving, but I needn't have worried. She came out and took me by the hand and sat me down. Putting her hand on my back, she said, "Listen, if I have said anything to you in anger, please don't be upset by it. The door of this home is always open for you, whenever you want." I thought it better not to waste any more time, so, without answering her, I quickly went in to fetch my things. I was putting them together when memsahib came up the stairs, slightly out of breath, and I understood that she wanted to see what I was taking away. She stood there as I packed, and then I took my things down to the rickshaw. I thought I would say good-bye to the dog but he was nowhere to be seen—perhaps they had kept him away because they did not want me making him un-happy. Then, without further ado, I left.

Slowly, I settled into my new house. The one thing that preyed on my mind all the time was how to find work—what would I do if I didn't manage to find a job? And so, once again, I began the same old treadmill: running from pillar to post in search of work. As well as this, I also tried to see if I could find a cheaper place to live. Would I be able to? I wasn't sure, but I was worried about having to pay the rent for the next month. A week and a half passed and I had not found anything. Meanwhile, my neighbors started to ask all sorts of questions: Why was I liv-ing alone? Did it not worry me? Where was my husband? Would I be able to manage? and so on . . . When they started asking me all these things, my instinct was always to run away and not talk to them. So I'd take the kids and run off, saying that I had to go out and find a job. But then I had to face endless questions about whether I had managed to find work or not! At those times my defense tactic was to start talking about the children.

There was a young man named Sunil who worked as a driver in the house opposite memsahib's. He was another one whom I'd asked to look for work for me, and one day I met him somewhere and he asked if I was still working in the house across the road. When I told him I had left that job a week and a half ago and was looking for work, he offered to help. He promised to keep his ear to the ground and let me know if anything came up. One afternoon, I was sleeping with the children when Sunil turned up and asked if I had found work. I said no. So he said, "Come with me, then."

"Where to?" I asked.

"Just come. If you need work, and once you've seen what there is to do, you can do the rest of the negotiations yourself."

So I went with him. He took me to a house and rang the bell and the sahib came out. Sunil said to him, "Here you are, sir, I have brought someone as you instructed me to."

"Are you Bengali?" the sahib asked me.

"Yes," I said.

"Well, then," he said, "the woman who works here is paid 800 rupees. I will see how you work and then decide on what to pay you."

"All right," I said, and asked what my hours would be.

"As early as possible, because I am an early riser."

"I have to cook and feed my children, so the earliest I can make it is around six or seven o'clock." I had the feeling the sahib wanted to talk a little more about money, so I hesitated as I was turning to leave but he just said, "All right, you can start to-morrow."

The next day when I came to work I saw a thirty-five- to forty-year-old widow heading into the same house to work. Sahib was outside watering the plants. The moment he saw me he went into the house and told the woman that she would have to leave, he had found someone else. She came out and started abusing me. I told her: "Look, I know nothing about all this. Had I known that there was someone already here, I wouldn't have said yes to the job. It's no use shouting at me like this. If you want, you go and tell the sahib that I am not willing to work like this, and then you can have your old job back."

But she did not do as I suggested and just went away, cursing

and screaming at me. Sahib then took me in and explained my
tasks to me. I worked hard and everyone in the house was surprised at my work. One day the sahib asked me how I managed to
squeeze in so much work in such little time and to do it so well.
"Where did you learn?" he asked. So I told him that I have no
problem doing domestic work because that's what I had done
since I was a child—with no mother at home, I was forced to take
on all the household tasks.

So this became my routine. I would go in the morning, finish all my work by the afternoon, and come back home. One
day the sahib asked me about my children and whether they
went to school or not. I told him that I wanted them to study
and was constantly on the lookout for something, but so much
depended on having the money to send them to school. I hadn't
given up hope, though, and I hoped that I would be able to do
so. Then one day he called me and said he wanted me to bring
my son and daughter to him. "There's a small school nearby, I'll
see what I can do there," he said, "Bring the children with you
in the morning, when you come, and leave them in the school.
Then they can go back with you when you go." So I began to do
this, and the children started to go to school. I'd leave them
there, come and work in the house, and in the afternoon, when
they came back to the house, the sahib always gave them something to eat.

Now I began to think about getting some extra work because
the money I was earning was not enough for all three of us. So I
asked sahib if he could help me, and he said he would look out
for work for me but that I should not go out looking for it myself.
But in any case, I needed a new place to live, and with this in
mind, I went to the neighborhood where my brother lived to see
if there were any places to rent there. I managed to find a place
where the rent was only five hundred rupees—the only trouble

was that there was no toilet in the house. But I thought, *If others can live like that, why can't I?* As usual, people had a lot of questions about me, and several of them tried to find out why I was alone, where I had come from, all the same things. Some of them were good to me, but many others said all kinds of things about me. Anyway, none of this concerned me and basically I kept myself a bit apart, waking in the morning and getting the children ready for school, after which I would lock up the house and go to work. Many people gossiped about how I would manage with only one house to work in, and to be honest, I was a bit concerned about this, too. Every day I would ask sahib if he had any news about possible work and he would say something or the other. I got the impression that he did not want me to work elsewhere. Perhaps he thought I would not be able to manage to do more than one job and if I did, my children would be neglected. Perhaps that was why one day he asked me, quite out of the blue, "Baby, how much do you spend in a month?" I was so embarrassed I did not say anything and he did not ask me again.

My routine was that I would wake in the morning and go more or less straight to work. There was no time to eat anything. At sahib's house, I would finish all the work and then go home to cook and clean. Sahib did not say anything, but I felt that he had compassion in his heart for me and sometimes in the morning when I went to his house he would be washing the dishes or sweeping the floor. I really liked working there. They appreciated my work, and no one ever scolded me or checked up on me. In the mornings, sahib always seemed happy to see me, and although he never said anything, I always felt that he was thinking: "What has this poor woman done that she had to leave her home and live alone like this?" He was concerned that I did not suffer anymore, and I felt sometimes that he wanted to say that to me, but that he hesitated to.

One day suddenly he asked me, "*Accha*, Baby, tell me what you do when you go home from here."

I said, "I cook for the children. Then I feed them and put them to sleep. In the evening, I take them out for a while and then when we come back I make them study and do their homework. Then they have to be fed again and put to bed, and then I get to sleep. In the morning, I get up and come here. That's my daily routine."

"So then how will you find time to do the other work you are looking for?"

"I'll have to manage it somehow, because without doing extra work I can't really survive."

"Well, what if I help you out, and you don't work anywhere else?"

I was very touched by his concern for me. I was thinking about this when he said, "What's the matter? You have not answered my question. What are you thinking about?"

I was silent: I just could not say anything.

He said, "Look, Baby: think of me as your father, brother, mother, friend, anything. Don't think you don't have anyone in the world. You can tell me anything you like." Then, after a moment, he added, "My children call me Tatush. You can also call me by that name." So I began to call him Tatush and he was very happy. He would say, "You're like my daughter, and you are now the daughter of this house. Don't ever think that you don't belong here." And indeed, everyone treated me like I was one of the family.

TATUSH HAD THREE CHILDREN, ALL YOUNG MEN, AND I had met only one of them, the youngest. If I was working in the kitchen and he wanted tea, he would come in and make his own and never ask me to do it for him. He spoke very little—not only with me, but with everyone. One day Tatush told me that his elder son was coming: "My elder son," he said, "meaning your older brother." I was really happy to hear this.

A few days later I was busy at work when Tatush called out to me. "Baby?" he said, "have you moved house yet?" I said yes. "But why did you not tell me? This is not right: you should have told me." And I thought: *He's right.* I don't know how or why I forgot, but I did. I realized that he was upset, but I could not understand how he had come to know that I had moved. Then he told me that Sunil had told him. And I was wondering how Sunil would have gotten to know, when Tatush said, "Sunil went to your old home to see you and found out that you had moved." He had met Sunil on his way to buy milk in the morning, which is how he had heard. "If Sunil had not told me, I would not have gotten to know," Tatush said. I felt really terrible. Then, a little later, Tatush asked: "When I called you just now, what were you doing?"

"I was dusting upstairs," I said.

"So go and finish your work."

I went back upstairs. In the upstairs room there were three cupboards full of books. Every time I saw them I wondered who read them. There were several books in Bengali, too, and I would sometimes dip into them. One day I was dusting in that room when Tatush came in. He saw that I was looking at a Bangla book, but he did not say anything then. The next day in the morning when I came to work and went in to give him his tea, he asked if I knew how to read and write. My heart sank and I did not know what to say so I mumbled something, pretended to laugh, and started to move away. He asked me again, "Can you read at all?"

"I won't lie," I said, "but what I know is like knowing nothing."

"But have you studied at all? Up to which class?"

"Till about the sixth or seventh." He seemed to fall into thought then and did not say anything more.

Next day when I came to work, he was smiling. Most of the time, he had a sort of half-smile on his face, and I often felt that he had no anger in his heart. He spoke slowly and gently, and always seemed to me to be like Sri Ramkrishna. Sometimes we would begin talking and would go on talking and he would tell me many things. I was standing there thinking these thoughts when he asked me, without any preamble, "So, Baby, do you remember the names of any writers you like?"

I looked at him and laughed. "Yes, there are some, like Rabindranath Tagore, Kazi Nasrul Islam, Sharatchandra, Satyendra Nath Dutt, Sukumar Rai. . . ." I don't know why I said these names, but Tatush put his hand on my head and looked at me in amazement. He looked as if he could not believe what he was hearing. Then he asked, "Do you like to read and write?"

I said, "Yes, I like it, but what's the point? There's no reading and writing for me now."

"But why not?" he said. "Look at me, I still read. Don't you know why all those books are there? If I can read, why can't you?" Then he said, "Come upstairs with me for a moment."

Upstairs he pulled a book out of the cupboard and said, "Tell me, what is this book called?"

I looked at the book and thought to myself: I can read this. But then I hesitated: What if I make a mistake and say the wrong thing? And then I told myself, So what? I'll then say I don't know how to read.

Tatush was watching me as these thoughts passed through my mind. "Go on," he urged me. "Read, read something at least." So

I blurted out, "*Amar Meyebela*, Taslima Nasrin." And Tatush said, "You were worried you'd make a mistake, weren't you?"

I laughed.

He said, "Here. Take this book home and read it if you like."

So I did. I would read a page or two every day. The people around—my neighbors—were very surprised and began to comment on my reading, but I did not really care. Every time I began to read, I found it a little difficult, but as I went on it became easier. One day Tatush asked me if I was managing to read the book I had taken. I said yes, and so he said, "I'm going to give you something that I want you to make use of. Just imagine that this is my work as well."

"What is it?" I asked.

He pulled out a notebook and pen from his writing table and said, "Here. Write something in this notebook. If you want, you can write your life story in this. Whatever has happened in your life ever since you can remember and you became aware of yourself. Whatever you remember up to now, write it down. Try to write a little bit every day."

I took the pen and notebook in my hand and as I began to think about what I would write, my thoughts ran away with me. Tatush said, "Why, what's wrong? What are you thinking about?" I started. I was so absorbed in my thoughts . . . and then I said, "I'm wondering if I will be able to write or not."

"Of course you will be able to write," he said, "whyever not? Go ahead: *write*." Pen and notebook in hand, I went home. I wrote two pages that day. I would write, then I would read Taslima Nasrin's book. In the morning when I went to work, Tatush asked me if I had written anything or not, and was really happy to hear that I had. "Excellent!" he said. "Write every day: you must do that."

Some days I would be so absorbed in my reading and writing that by the time I looked up from my books, everyone around was well into their second sleep. Sometimes they would wake to find me still at work. And in the morning someone or the other would ask me, "So, what is it that keeps you awake? Why do you read so much?" I tried to fob them off: their questions made me unhappy. I was not comfortable in my house and wanted to leave it. All the time I was hoping to be able to find another place that was better than this one. It was very inconvenient to have to share a bathroom with four other families. In the morning you had to queue up to use it. And we were not allowed to use it to shit, we had to go out into the fields where there were pigs and other animals, so it was not very easy. Boys and girls, the young and old, we all had to carry our bottles of water and go off into the fields.

Tatush had once asked me if the place I stayed in had a bathroom. He had suggested I use the bathroom upstairs in his home. So then I began to use it, and I would bathe there before going home. Sometimes when I got home late my landlady would demand to know why I was so late, and that made me very angry. I thought, *What business is it of hers?* I am not tied to her and she has no control over my life. I pay my rent and that is all they should be concerned about. Why then are these people so interested in what I do? After all, I so rarely went out anywhere. The moment I got home I would finish my chores and settle down to my reading and writing. The only thing I did was to occasionally go and visit a friend of mine, Savita. She was my friend from the old house I had worked in and there were times when I was late coming back from her place. This was hardly a crime, but my landlady was so nosy and interfering that even when I went to buy vegetables and provisions she would want to know where I had been. "Where do you *go* every day?" she would ask. "You should not go out so much."

Would it have made a difference if my husband had been with me, I wondered? When we were together there were still questions, and being with him was no different from my being alone. And if people talked then, when he was with me, how could I hope to shut them up if I was alone with just my children? People talked about my being alone, living in a rented house, and having just the children with me. And because of this, many thought I was fair game and I faced quite a bit of harassment. Some men would make the excuse that they wanted water to drink and would push their way into my home. Or if I went somewhere with the children, they'd follow me and try to force me to talk to them. But once I got to Tatush's home and began talking to him, I would forget all this. Tatush had some friends in Kolkata and Delhi and he had told them about my reading and writing. They took a real interest and that made me very happy.

One day when I was at home with the children, the landlord's elder son came by. I asked him to come in and sit down and he just parked himself there, without making any move to go. He began to talk and didn't seem to want to stop. The things he said were very embarrassing and I could not even bring myself to reply to them. Nor could I ask him to go, or even leave myself. He had sat himself down by the front door so that if I wanted to get out, I would have to brush past him. I understood very well what it was he wanted, although I had to pretend innocence. It was clear from what he said that if I wanted peace of mind, I would have to find myself another place to live. If I wanted to stay on in this house, I'd have to make sure he was happy, and I knew what *that* meant. I felt a tremendous sense of resignation and despair—if there was no man in the house, did that mean I would have to listen to anyone who decided he had a right over my life? I thought I would find a new home the very next day, and began to hunt again.

ONE DAY, AS I WAS COMING BACK FROM WORK, MY CHILdren came up to me crying. They told me that our house had been broken down. I screamed, "How could this be? Who has done this?" When we got home, I saw that they had thrown everything out on the street. I sat down there with my head in my hands. What was I to do now? Where were we to go? How would I find a new place so soon, at this time of the day? The children and I sat down there and wept.

It wasn't only my house that had been broken down. Many houses in the neighbourhood had suffered the same fate, but in each of them there was a man—a father, a husband, a brother. I had nobody. That's why my things were still scattered all around while the other occupants had at least collected and put their things in one place, and someone or the other had headed off to look for a new place to live. There were a few people who had stayed behind—a handful of them who cared for my children and were sorry to see us in such a state. I could not stop crying, and seeing me cry, my children also began to weep. I really felt at the time that I had no one in the world to call my own, no one who could come to my help. I had two brothers who lived just across the road. They knew where I was, they also knew that all the houses in that area had been broken down—that kind of news spreads quickly. But there was not a sign of them. I thought about my mother. Had she been there, perhaps there would have been someone to care for me. How much more sorrow would I have to bear?

There was no hunting for a new house that day. We sat there until the evening, when a neighbor, Bhola-da, came. He was a Muslim and belonged to the same area as us. He knew my father and my brothers and he was very fond of my children. "How will you stay here all night alone?" he asked, sitting down next to us. We spent the night in that open, dirty place, wet with the dew falling on us, and somehow night turned into day. No one slept that night.

In the morning Bhola-da said to me, "Why don't you talk to the sahib in the house you are working in?" *He is right,* I thought, *Tatush had said he could give me a place to stay.* But then I said to Bhola-da, "Please, why don't you come and talk to him? I will not have the courage to do so." Bhola-da agreed: "All right. Let's go."

When we got to the house, he waited outside while I went in. Tatush was reading the papers. He took one look at me and said, "What is it, Baby? Why are you looking so pale and drawn? You don't look like this normally." I told him everything: how the bulldozers had destroyed all our homes, how the children and I had had to spend the night outside in the damp. "There's a man I know who has come with us," I said. "He's waiting outside and wants to talk to you." Tatush went outside and talked to Bhola-da.

When he came back in he asked me, "Why on earth did you not come here last night? Why did you wait till the morning? And why spend the night outside with the children? You should have come straightaway. Anyway, now tell me, when are you coming?"

"Whenever you say."

"Right now," Tatush said.

I agreed, and went back and brought my things in a rickshaw. I was thinking how Tatush had not hesitated even a moment to ask me to come.

When I returned, Tatush had emptied out a room on the roof of his house for me. I put my things there and went down to cook his lunch. He came up to look and then came to me and said, "You needn't cook today if you don't want to, there's plenty of food downstairs."

"That doesn't matter," I said. "Your son and the others can eat that later.

"Do you think you will be able to make some hot rotis at night?" Tatush asked. "Up until now there's been no one to cook the evening meal. I normally eat the same thing at night that you cook in the morning. But now that you are here, do you think you can give me hot food at night as well?"

Now I began to cook and work downstairs and I did everything. No one had to tell me what to do: I just worked. Sometimes Tatush would say to me, "Baby, how can you do so much work? You're working all the time. Come and sit and talk to me sometimes." And then I'd sit down and talk to him and he would ask, "Have your children eaten yet? Have you given them lunch? Go upstairs and feed them, and then come down and have your own meal. Take a bit of milk from here for them." After coming to Tatush's house, my children began to get a half-liter of milk every day.

One day Tatush said to me, "You know, Baby, there have been other women who have worked in this house, but I have not found a girl like you. You must never think you are in this house only as a domestic worker. Think of this house as your own. I have no daughter, so I think of you as my daughter." I thought: *What a nice thing to say!* Only I knew how happy I was after I came into this home. Tatush took so much care of me, and if ever I felt unwell, he would come and help out with the work and would be very concerned for my health. He would force me to go to the doctor, then get the prescribed medicines for me and ensure that I took them. If I demurred, he would force me to take them, insisting that I had to listen to him. If one of my children was ill, he would do the same. I had never met anyone who treated their home workers so well. I lacked for nothing in that home—soap, food, clothes, medicines, everything was there for me. I thought, *I have worked in so many homes, but never have I been in a place where everyone is so kind to me.* It was as if I was everything in that house.

I had everything I needed here, but even so, every now and again I felt sad. It was two months since I had seen my elder son. Perhaps Tatush understood my sorrow, for one day he asked me, "Baby, where does your elder son stay? Why don't you go to see him sometime?" He asked me once, twice, three times, and I had no answer to give him. Then, without looking him in the eye, I told him that I did not even know where my son was. "What?" he exclaimed, "You don't know where he is? How can that be?"

So I told him how the people who had taken him away had lived close to where I was and they had told me roughly where he was but I had no idea of the house number, the correct address, or anything like that. I'd gone to each of the houses whose numbers they gave me, not once but several times, but everywhere I drew a blank. The only thing I knew was that his employer had a medicine shop close by—but I had not been able to trace that, either. Tatush was concerned—there were many medicine shops in that neighborhood—but he did not say anything at that time.

The next morning he called me in and told me that when they were taking my son away with them, I should have actually spoken to him and explained our circumstances so that he'd not feel abandoned, and I should have also checked on where they were taking him. That way, I could've at least kept in touch with him. "You know," he said, "anything could have happened and you would not have known." I had nothing to say. After that he left the house without saying anything to me and came back some three hours later. The moment he returned, he got on the phone. I heard him talking to someone and then he called out to me, "Baby, Baby! Come here." I went in and he continued to talk on the phone while I waited, then he handed the phone to me and said, "Here. Talk."

I asked, "Who is it? Who should I talk to?"

He said, "Just talk."

I took the phone. Someone was saying, "Hello? Hello?" but I couldn't make out who it was, so I held the phone a little away from my ear and asked Tatush who it was. He said, "Don't you know your own son?" I was really taken aback. My son! I put the phone to my ear again and said "Beta, Beta, it's your mother."

He said, "Ma? Is that you?"

I said, "Yes, son, yes, it's me, Baby. How are you, my son?"

"I'm fine, Ma," he said, "absolutely fine. I am well here, don't worry about me."

I thought, *My boy has grown up now, his voice has changed so much!* How he has changed in such a short while! I wanted very much to see him. Tatush understood this, and he asked me if that was what I wanted to do. I said, "Yes, that would be wonderful!" So he said, "When do you want to go?"

"Whenever you say," I replied.

When a few days later I went to see my son, I found him watering plants outside the house where he worked. I don't know why, but I did not feel he was happy. But there was nothing I could do. He came up to me and was so happy to see his little brother and sister. When we were about to leave, he looked really sad. I resolved then that I would somehow bring him to live with me. I'm sure Tatush understood all this because every now and

again he would insist I call my son to ask after him. But whenever I did, my son wanted to know my address to find out where
I lived and I always gave him insufficient information because I
did not want him turn up at Tatush's house unannounced. What
would I do then? Tatush would sometimes say he had not seen a
boy like him and I wondered what he meant—perhaps he did
not feel he could trust him. Why did he never ask me to bring
my boy over sometime, even for a short while? But I did not say
anything to him.

And then one day Tatush said, "Baby, why don't you bring
your son here for a few days for Kali Puja?" I was so happy. Then
he said, "You know, you should also look for work for him somewhere here so that he can also study alongside. Do you know,
Baby, that it is illegal for children to work?" I thought I would like
nothing better than to have him live with us, but how could I
manage in the same house with three children? So I said to Tatush,
"You had said I should find extra work in the neighborhood for
an hour or two. Perhaps I should do that?"

"What's the use of that, Baby? You'll work in one place and
then come and work here and you will make yourself ill. You have
to take care of your health."

I was so touched by Tatush's words. I thought that even my father had not advised me like this and shown such concern for me.
Tatush must have been my father in my previous life, otherwise
why would he worry so much about what was good for me and
what was not? After a little while he said, "I'd given you some writing work and some reading to do. Have you made any progress
with that? It would be better for you to focus on that: the time will
be well spent. One day this will come in useful. You don't need to
do anything else, Baby: just focus on your reading and writing.
There's no need to run around so much. For the moment, leave
things as they are. And then, just think how much pleasure your

writing gives to my friends who've been reading your work. They're always encouraging you to write and if they find out that instead of writing you are running around looking for work, they will blame me!"

A few days later, Tatush asked me to bring my son to the house. "I don't like his working like this at all. If he continues to work in other people's houses at this age, what will become of him? His life will be destroyed. I am a teacher, Baby, and I cannot stand to see a young person's life ruined. Go over today and bring him here."

I went and fetched my son the same day. Tatush now began to look for a good place where he could work and where he would have time to study as well. It wasn't easy to find such a place, of course. Now I had all three children with me—but I was still not happy. I thought, Tatush is already doing so much for us, how much more could I expect him to do? I did not want to feel I was exploiting him, so I decided that until such time as my son was with me, I would be a little thrifty and I would not, for example, cook any extra quantities of food.

Tatush understood that I was concerned about food. He began to insist that I eat with him, and sometimes he even went so far as to put food on a plate for me and insist that I eat. This family gave me so much happiness. I had worked in so many houses, but nowhere had I found people like this. Previous to this, the houses in which I had worked had paid me the monthly wage, but here there was nothing like that. Tatush had said to me, "Baby, don't think that I am paying you a salary. Just look on this money as your pocket money!"

One day Tatush suggested I go to the park for a while in the evenings and take the children with me. I did as he suggested and started to go to the park every day. There were many Bengali women who came to the park with the children they had charge of. And some began to ask me questions: Are you Bengali? Are you married? Where is your husband? and so on. There were also some young boys and often they tried to talk to me, or to be nice to my children so that they could then open up a conversation. I did not talk much to these people—although if someone came up to you and started talking it was difficult to not reply—and I would not tell them anything about myself. I understood their motives well enough. Tatush had also advised me not to talk to people I did not know. He was right, because often such people would ask questions in order to wheedle out information that you did not want to give them, and they would ask them in such a roundabout way that you wouldn't even realize until it was too late. This was one reason that I was not so keen to go out.

One day in the park I saw a young girl with a child. I'd seen her around for a few days. She did not talk to anyone in the park and was always alone. But there were some young boys who passed all sorts of remarks about her. She must have been around twenty or twenty-two and it was clear that she was not married. I felt very sorry for her. I wondered how her parents could have sent her so far away to work. I spoke to her one day and she was so happy to respond. I asked if she was Bengali and she said yes and told me her name: Suniti. We became good friends. We'd meet in the park every day and if we did not manage to meet one day, we really missed each other. Suniti had lost both her parents early—her mother died in childbirth when Suniti was born and she had been brought up by her grandmother and her uncle. I felt very sorry for her. I knew what it was like to grow up without a mother. I met Suniti the day before she left for home and we did not know that she would be gone the next day. She had told me she would give me her address but that did not happen. Suddenly one day she did not come to the park anymore—I had taken my address along but I had no idea at all that she had already gone. After that day I did not see her again and a couple of days later I saw that the child she used to bring to the park was with someone else. That was when I realized she was gone. I thought she probably was not able to find time to meet me, and after all, what could she do? She was at the mercy of the people she worked for.

After Suniti left I stopped going to the park and used my time to read and write. When I had written a fair amount, Tatush took my papers, had them photocopied, and sent them to a friend in Kolkata. Then one day he said to me, "Baby, there's a letter for you." I was surprised. A letter! Who could be writing to me? Tatush then told me that it was from his friend in Kolkata, so I asked him to read it out to me.

"Dear Baby," it said, "I cannot tell you how happy I was to read your manuscript. How did you learn to write so well? Your writing is excellent and your Tatush has really found a jewel in you. I'm only sorry I can't write to you in Bengali. I can read Bengali but I can't write it. I am a year older than your Tatush. I would like to be able to learn Bengali but now there is no time. Please continue to read and write in Bangla. Many of my friends wanted to read your story and I have shown it to them. One of my friends would like to have your story published in a paper but first you must bring it to some sort of conclusion. And I want to tell you that you must never stop writing. Remember that God has placed you on this earth to write. My blessings are with you."

I was really dumbstruck. What had I written to merit this kind of response? I wondered. My writing was a bit crude, but they still liked it. I asked Tatush why they liked my writing so much and he said, "You won't understand." And this was true! I really did not understand. I think God did not give me the power to understand, but I still wanted to. Then Tatush told me not to bother about all this, just keep doing your work, do your reading and writing and the understanding will come one day by itself.

But where was the time to read and write? At home there were not only Arjun-da, Sukhdeep-da, and Raman-da but their friends Rajat-da, Rahul-da, and Sumit-da, who came and went. They were all really kind to me: how could I not give them dinner and lunch and just go off and write? One day I got so absorbed in talking to Tatush about my reading and writing that a funny thing happened. Normally I would put the food on the table for Sukhdeep-da and Raman-da, and leave the plate upturned to keep off any flies. Raman-da came back from work and he was starving so he went straight to the table and without noticing that the plate was upside-down, served himself. Naturally, the vegetables and the dal started sliding off the plate onto the tablecloth. Suddenly he noticed what he was doing and started laughing loudly. Tatush and I were wondering who he was talking to, since there was no one else in the house. Then I went in to see and found him laughing hysterically at what he had done. At first I could not understand, and then, when I did, I could not help laughing either. Tatush joined us and very soon he, too, was in splits. Then Tatush said to me, "Baby, you have not yet replied to the letter my friend wrote you, and it's been so many days."

"Letter?" I said. "But I don't know how to write letters!"

"Why not?" Tatush said. "Just write however you want to, it will come right in the end."

I thought about it. I had never written to anyone. How would I do it? What would I write? And I make mistakes—I was also worried about this. I asked Tatush, how should I address him? He said: however you like. So I thought I would call him Jethu and I wrote to him. I don't know what kind of letter I wrote, but I got a reply:

"Dear Baby," it said, "I got your letter a few days ago and was very happy and have been wondering what to write. Some days ago I went to the book market here. There, they sell books like they sell fish. I wanted to buy up the whole market and send all those books to you. I'm very pleased to know that the second part of your story is now complete. You are quite right to say that your Tatush and I have been worried about your writing and the reason for our worry is that we want your work to be published and we have been wondering how this can be done. Your Tatush must have told you about Ashapurna Devi, the writer who used to finish all her housework and then write in secret. She only spoke Bengali and she never stepped outside her house. Your Tatush and I, who do not have even an inch of writing in us, know a little about this world of writing and our hope is that you will be the new Ashapurna Devi. How far have you got with the third part? Your Jethu."

This was how Jethu encouraged me. And he was not alone in this. In Delhi, Tatush had another friend, Ramesh Babu. One day he said to me on the phone, "Baby, a friend of mine liked what you have written very much. He said it was like Anne Frank's diary."

"Who is this Anne Frank?" I asked.

Tatush told me about her and brought me a newspaper that had some sections of her diary in it. These he read out to me and I felt a great sense of compassion for the young girl.

In Kolkata, Jethu had a friend, Sharmila-di, a teacher who was from the same area as I was. She was also a great friend of mine and used to write to me often. Reading her letters, I often wanted to talk to her, play with her, and jump about because I felt very close to her in spirit.

One day, while cleaning an almirah upstairs, I came across a photo album. I opened it to look inside and found many pictures there of Arjun-da and his friends. In one picture I saw Jethu, with Sharmila-di on one side and Arjun-da on the other. In another was Jethu with Sharmila-di and Sukhdeep-da. So far I had not met Jethu or Sharmila-di in person: these photos were the only time I had seen them. Whenever Sharmila-di wrote to me, she included all sorts of notepaper cut in different shapes in her letter for my reply. We talked of so many things in our letters, and sometimes I wondered if we would have as much to talk about if we met. Jethu had a Bengali friend, Anand, and he also wrote to me. He said, "I liked your writing very much. This kind of writing is very difficult to do. Not everyone has the skill to be able to delve into so many diverse memories and render them so simply, so movingly. Do not ever stop doing this. If you continue to work like this, one day you may also be able to touch on many other issues—women's oppression, their difficulties . . . you have begun to do this so well. My blessings are with you."

Anand Babu also sent me something he had written. I read it with great interest. I can't say I understood all of it, and Tatush also patiently explained some things to me. But whatever I understood, I liked. Tatush also sent my writing to some of his other friends. But despite all the encouragement and kind words I received from all these people, I was still unsure of myself: Would I be able to write? Would I live up to their expectations?

ONE DAY, OUT OF THE BLUE, MY FATHER CAME TO SEE US. I was cooking when I looked out of the kitchen window and saw someone come up to the house on a cycle. I did not recognize him. He rang the bell and it took me some time to go out and open the door. When I went out, he said, "How are you, child?"

"Baba!" I screamed. "What have you done to yourself? Why are you so thin?"

"Nothing's happened to me, Beta. I am perfectly all right. How are the children?"

"They're well. Everything is all right, the children are at school right now."

I ran in and told Tatush that my father had come and he asked me to call him in, make him sit down, offer him something to eat. I brought him to my room and asked if he wanted a cup of tea. "No," he said, "it's too hot."

So I quickly made a glass of sherbet and offered that to him. He took it and asked, "What about you? Why don't you drink some?"

"I've just had a cup of tea," I told him. I asked him how Ma was. "She is all right," he said. "She remembers you often." And I thought, *Yes, it's been a long time, two years.* But I also thought, If I go there for a couple of days, all the old battles will begin again. I was not prepared to go through that again. One thing that had become clear to me by this time was that man or woman, everyone was basically concerned about themselves and about having enough to eat. Had I understood this wisdom earlier, I would not have had to suffer so much.

For a while we chatted about this and that—all sorts of things—and then I asked Baba how everyone was in Kolkata. How was my brother, and how was Ma? Baba said, "Ma? Your ma? Do you mean you haven't heard?" He looked at me for a long moment. Perhaps he was wondering how to tell me, and worrying that I would not be able to take it. Should I tell her, he must have wondered, can she take the truth? Should I tell her that her mother is dead? I thought I saw these thoughts passing through his mind. I cried, "Baba!" and he started. I was sure by now that my mother was dead. "What happened? Is Ma all right?"

"Your Ma?" he said, "Your Ma has been dead these six or seven years. Did your brother not tell you?"

"No, no one told me," I said, sobbing. *And even if they had,* I thought, *what could I have done?* I'd heard once that she was in the hospital—she must have died that time because there was no news of her after that. I thought, *Everyone knows everything except me.* My brother, his children and family . . . they all live so close by but no one thinks I need to be told anything. I'd visited their home so often, but no one had so much as mentioned that Ma was ill or that she had passed away. And all this time I had been planning to visit her. I had heard that when she was ill in hospital, my younger brother had gone to Baba and asked him to visit her in hospital, but Baba did not go. And why should he? He didn't need Ma for anything. I thought he must have known that she would not survive but he did not go. He could have done this as a last gesture for her, but he did not. My younger brother had to do her last rites on his own; even my older brother and his family apparently got to know much later. And I heard only now.

Baba asked me where my elder son was. I told him he was working nearby and Baba asked if we could go and see him. So we went. My son was so happy to see him, he cried out, "*Arre,* Dadu!" and touched his feet. Then he immediately asked, "How is my Baba?"

"He is all right. I asked him to come with me but he didn't." Baba looked at my son and his eyes filled with tears. "How you people have grown up," he said, "and you're doing well. I am so happy for you." Then he turned and said to me, "Now you will not have any problem, child, your son has grown up and he will look after you. Just wait and see: one day your troubles will be over and your son will be there standing by you." Then he blessed my boy. "Stay well, son," he said and came back with me. As he prepared to leave our home, Tatush came out and said to Baba, "Don't worry about your daughter, she will be all right."

"Now that she is with you, I have no worries at all. I know she will be all right." Then he left. He had heard from someone that I was now writing, and he was very happy to hear this. Unlike earlier times when he did not even bother with me, now he was anxious to know about my writing and would often call to ask. He always asked if I wanted to come back and immediately added that if I did not want to stay I could come right back. But I had no desire to go.

STILL, I WAS VERY SAD AFTER BABA WENT. I WISHED I HAD seen my mother before she died. I worried about Baba's health. Jethu and Sharmila had written me many letters to which I had not responded, and these sat on my head like another worry. Finally, one day, I decided that I must at least write back to them and perhaps that would make me feel better, so I collected all the letters and sat myself down. Then I thought of reading them again once before writing back. I began with Jethu's letters and started reading them as I would a story. In one of them he said, "Tatush had told you to consult a dictionary, and he is right, you must do so. That way, you will make fewer mistakes and will find it easier to write letters. It does not matter if you do make mistakes. Don't let that put you off. You will learn from these to write well. It is no bad thing to keep trying. Don't let your story get lost in sleep like your Tatush does! In the new year, I want you to write a lot more and to be well and healthy. I like your writing very much and I be-

lieve that others will like it too. I am sending you this essay at the
suggestion of my friend, Anand. You cannot imagine how much
pleasure your writing has given your Jethu and your Tatush and
how much it has made us think. The best thing is that now you do
not seem to find the writing as difficult as you used to. Have you
read anything else by Ashapurna Devi? Sometimes, earlier, I
found your writing a bit difficult but now it is very fluent. Now,
while reading, I want to pat you on the back and say *shabaash*:
well done! If a writer starts worrying about what he or she has
left out or forgotten, they might not be able to write even a single
line. So the best thing to do is just to write, and then look at your
writing later and clean it up. And then, you leave the further
cleaning to those whose job it is to read and write, like editors. If
you want to become a writer, the only way to do so is to determine
to sit down and write and then to do so. This is something you
have also understood. Your Tatush is right in telling you that if
you make mistakes, don't worry: just write." The more letters I
read from Jethu, the more I felt encouraged to write.

Sharmila's letters were very different. She wrote to me in
Hindi. I thought she must have a girl working in her home just
like me. Does she deal with her in the same way as she does with
me? She did not treat me like domestic help at all: rather, it was as
if we were friends. Tatush would read her letters out to me and I
would then copy them down in my broken Bengali and read them
again later when I felt low. She said, "Baby, think about why you
are so upset with your father. Put yourself in his shoes for once
and see how you feel. Even if you feel you cannot forgive him, you
must do so. We must forgive people even if we don't like them . . .
If you come here, we'll both dress up and dance and sing. I like
dressing up sometimes and when you are here, you dress up for
me and I will for you. When we meet each other we will laugh to
our heart's content, even if there is nothing to laugh about, we'll

laugh. Baby, do you feel surprised when someone tells you how much they like your writing? And do you wonder how your difficult, hard life has suddenly become transformed into such beautiful prose?"

I was amused at her asking me about dressing up because I have never liked to dress up. I had seen so many girls and women who, the moment they thought they were going out, would pull out powder, lipstick, comb, *sindoor* . . . they'd put on their saris and then preen in front of the mirror and ask their friends how they looked.

EVERY MORNING I READ THE PAPERS. I DO NOT KNOW English but I still looked at the English papers, sometimes just at the pictures, and I would ask Tatush to explain them to me. Then Tatush would say, "Try to read the words that are below the pictures." I'd then read the letters, one by one, and Tatush would keep nodding or saying, *Hmm, hmm.* After I finished reading the characters, Tatush would pronounce the whole word and explain its meaning to me. Sometimes I had so many questions for him that he could not manage to read the newspaper himself. Perhaps that was why sometimes he would say to me, "Baby, don't you need to send the children to school?"

"Yes, but there is still time," I'd say.

"When will you go? You'll be late: you'd better go now."

And then I would get up and go. Sending the children to school was not the only task I had to do: there was so much else. The moment Arjun-da woke up, for example, I had to get breakfast and some food ready for him. He liked to eat special things and he did not like cold rotis, so they had to be made fresh each time. I did not mind this: I like cooking for people and feeding them, and even when I was with my husband, any time I made something new, I would share it with everyone around. Perhaps that was what made him so unhappy with me!

I also liked looking at cookery books as much as I liked reading books and poems and stories. Reading the newspaper had become like an addiction and everything that Tatush read to me or told me about from the newspaper was like a new discovery for me. Perhaps this was why I waited at the gate every morning for the papers to come.

One day I was late waking up. When I came down I saw that Tatush had fetched the papers and he was reading them. I went quickly to the kitchen to make tea. I gave him his tea and picked up the other paper and started to look at the pictures. Tatush said, "Where is your tea? Go and fetch it." I brought the tea and stood there drinking it, and he said, "Why are you standing? Sit down."

I sat down in a chair, put my glass of tea down on the table, and began to look at the paper again. Tatush said, "Baby, it has been a year since you came to this house. Tell me, how do you feel about this? What is it that you like and what don't you like? What do you think you have learned since you came here?" And then he went back to his paper.

Baby thought to herself, Is this any kind of question? She did not give him an answer. She went and stood by the window and looked out at the sky. Baby remembered her mother and thought how much she had wanted that her children learn to read and write and lead a good life. She did not manage to study herself, but as long as she was with her children, she never stopped urging them to do so. Had she been alive today and seen that her Baby was able to read and was learning to do more, how happy she would have been. Baby looked at the sky as if searching for her mother, as if to say to her, "Ma, come and see once, I still want to read and write, I want my children to read and write. They need

your blessings, Ma." Baby was talking to her mother, and her face
was wet with tears, her shirt damp as they slid down her chest and
fell to the ground.

THE TEA HAD GONE COLD. SUDDENLY BABY HEARD FOOT-
steps and started. She looked up and saw Arjun-da was awake
and was coming down the stairs. "You people are drinking tea
already?" he said. "Where's mine?" She headed off to the kitchen
to make tea when someone rang the bell at the gate. Outside was
a boy from a neighboring house. He had a parcel that he gave to
her, saying, "This came for you yesterday. It was delivered to our
house by mistake."

She took the packet and gave it to Tatush. But Tatush handed
it back. "This is for you. Here, take it—see what's inside." She
took the packet and went into the kitchen and put the water to
boil for Arjun-da's tea. Then she opened the packet. There was
a magazine inside. She started to turn the pages when her own
name jumped out at her. Surprised, she looked again, and it was
true, it was there! The words said: *Aalo Aandhari*, Baby Halder!*
Her heart leaped for joy! It was as if it had begun to turn cart-
wheels. In the middle of all this she remembered Jethu's story
about Ashapurna Devi writing after doing all her other housework. She thought, Jethu was right, one can write along with
doing household work.

Suddenly she noticed that the water had nearly boiled dry!
She quickly made the tea and gave it to Arjun-da, and then ran
upstairs to her children, shouting, "Look! Look! I have something
to show you, *look* . . ." The children came running and she said to

---

* *Aalo Aandhari* (*From Darkness to Light*) is the title of Baby Halder's book in
Hindi and Bengali.

them, "*See!* Tell me what is written here." Her daughter hesitat-
ingly read each letter and made out the words: *Aalo Aandhari*,
Baby Halder . . . "Ma! Your name in a *book!!*" Both children
began to laugh for joy. She looked at them and tenderness welled
up in her heart. She took them into her arms and held them close.
And suddenly, the thought came to her that she had forgotten
something: "Let me go, let me go!" she said to the children, "I'll
be back, right away!" and she ran downstairs. How silly I am! she
thought, I saw my name in the magazine and forgot everything!
She came downstairs and knelt down to touch Tatush's feet. He
put his hand on her head and blessed her.